The Adventures of M. James

Michael James, 1942

The Adventures of M. James

A Sailor's Diary

aboard the

U.S.S. MONTEREY, CVL-26

WORLD WAR II

Pacific Ocean
September 15, 1943 to October 19, 1945

Atlantic Ocean
November 18, 1945 to January 1, 1946

by

Michael James

Foreword by Anne D. Rogers

TURN OF THE SCREW PRESS • DUBLIN, NEW HAMPSHIRE

2005

Grateful acknowledgement is made to USS *Monterey* shipmates Sig Alman, Ned Bishop, Orlan Lorton and William Terheun, with special thanks to Frank Slater, for all their inspiration and support of this publication; to Sarah F. Bauhan, Edie Clark and Marne Goodrich for their generous publishing and editorial advice; to the staff of the Gerald R. Ford Library for providing many photographs; and to the following for permission to reprint previously published material:

THE ILLUSTRATED LONDON NEWS: 'A Map of American and British Strongholds Confronting Japan' illustration by G.F. Morrell, F.R.G.S., F.R.A.S., from the 25 October 1941 issue of *The Illustrated London News*, page 533. Reprinted by permission of The Illustrated London News Picture Library.

CREATORS SYNDICATE, INC.: 'Tall Tale Makes Big Waves' column by Ann Landers from the 2 May 1994 issue of *The Boston Globe*. Reprinted by permission of Esther P. Lederer Trust and Creators Syndicate, Inc.

Official U.S. Navy, Marine Corps. and Coast Guard photographs appearing in this publication are located in the collections of the U.S. National Archives and Records Administration, College Park, Maryland.

Cover photo: USS *Monterey* in action, Pacific Ocean, 1944, courtesy of the Gerald R. Ford Library.
Cover inset: photo of the author taken by his father during his first leave from the Navy, 1942.
Title page illustration: logo for USS *Monterey* newsletter drawn by the author, 1944.
Jacket design by Henry James

Library of Congress Cataloging-in-Publication Data

James, Michael, 1923–
The adventures of M. James : a sailor's diary aboard the U.S.S. Monterey, CVL-26 World War II : Pacific Ocean, September 15, 1943 to October 19, 1945 : Atlantic Ocean, November 18, 1945 to January 1, 1946 / by Michael James ; foreword by Anne D. Rogers.
p. cm.
Summary: "A World War II diary written during the height of Naval operations in the Pacific by a young sailor aboard the USS Monterey, CVL-26, from 1943 to 1946"—Provided by publisher.

ISBN 0-9762046-2-2 (alk. paper)

1. James, Michael, 1923—Diaries. 2. Monterey (Aircraft carrier) 3. World War, 1939–1945—Naval operations, American. 4. World War, 1939–1945—Campaigns—Pacific Ocean. 5. World War, 1939–1945—Campaigns—Atlantic Ocean. 6. World War, 1939–1945—Personal narratives, American. 7. United States. Navy—Aerographers—Diaries. I. Title.
D774.M66J36 2005
940.54'5973'092—dc22

2005005005

TURN OF THE SCREW PRESS
P.O. BOX 135
DUBLIN, NEW HAMPSHIRE
03444

visit us at www.turnofthescrewpress.com

PRINTED AND BOUND IN THE UNITED STATES OF AMERICA

TO MY BROTHERS SANDY AND DANNY,

HEROES BEYOND MEASURE.

WW II

My brother Sandy, 1918–1995

U.S. Marine, 4th Division

Fought on Saipan, Tinian, Kwajalein and Iwo Jima

My brother Danny, 1922–1955

U.S. Merchant Marine

Photo taken by my father following Danny's Murmansk runs across the North Atlantic, transporting dynamite, from February through May of 1942. His next ship was the S.S. *Lahaina*, first one to be sunk after Pearl Harbor on December 11, 1942.

THE DEMOCRACIES' NET AROUND JAPAN: U.S. AND BRITISH BASES.

Drawn by G. F. Morrell, F.R.G.S., F.R.A.S.

U.S. STRATEGIC PACIFIC SITES: A MAP OF AMERICAN AND BRITISH STRONGHOLDS CONFRONTING JAPAN.

Contents

Foreword

THE DIARY of Michael James, written (illegally) while he was an aerographer aboard the carrier *Monterey* during the height of Pacific operations in World War II to its conclusion at Hiroshima, is a unique document. The ingredients of Solzenitzen's *A Day in the Life of Ivan Denizovitch*, *Mister Roberts'* Ensign Pulver, and Remarque's *All Quiet on the Western Front* are all there, yet presented as only a naive, charming, eager, funny, sensitive young enlisted man could record them, minute by minute, on the spot.

The author is not looking back, he is not developing a theme; he is writing neither a war thriller, an anti-war treatise, nor yet a psychological portrait of a young man at war. Paradoxically, he has written all three. Constipation, the death of shipmates, and worms in the bread all receive equal billing in one day's entry. The beauty of ignited Japanese planes is described with elation in the same paragraph as a brief but poignant awareness that pilots, too, must have families. As a ringleader in a satire on a captain (refrain: "In a pig's ass he does"), young James comments on the affair's cruelty, but continues, "he deserved it."

For the historian, the psychologist, the military buff, the pacifist, the lover of humor, the philosopher, or the person who merely reads for entertainment, Michael James' War Diary (1943 to 1946) is mandatory reading. For this reviewer it confirms, as no impassioned pacifistic tract could, the senseless, mindless idiocy of war. By his very involvement, excitement and acceptance, despite his unusual sensitivity, the young sailor shows us with every entry how and why there will always be war, and why the trusting, fresh, idealistic young as well as the deprived and the dullards, are the basic ingredients of war.

James has not, as his grandfather William James did in his "Moral Equivalent of War," written a reasoned plea for peace. He has, however, inadvertently given a picture of war, its pernicious, self-propagating, universally accepted and therefore, pervasively evil essence, which haunts one long after the diary is finished.

Anne D. Rogers, 1926–1991
Deerfield, Massachusetts

Author's Note

THIS JOURNAL is not intended to be a definitive account of America's war in the Pacific. In fact, a critical reading of the thing would serve an historian ill. This is not to say the truth has ever been deliberately twisted. It's just that inaccuracies do turn up from time to time; errors of youth, distraction, ignorance, and haste. What matters here is not the fact that on September 21, 1944, an eight-ship convoy was sighted off Corregidor Bay (there may have been nine), but rather, the *flavor* of the thing, its tone.

This, then, is as I saw it at the time.

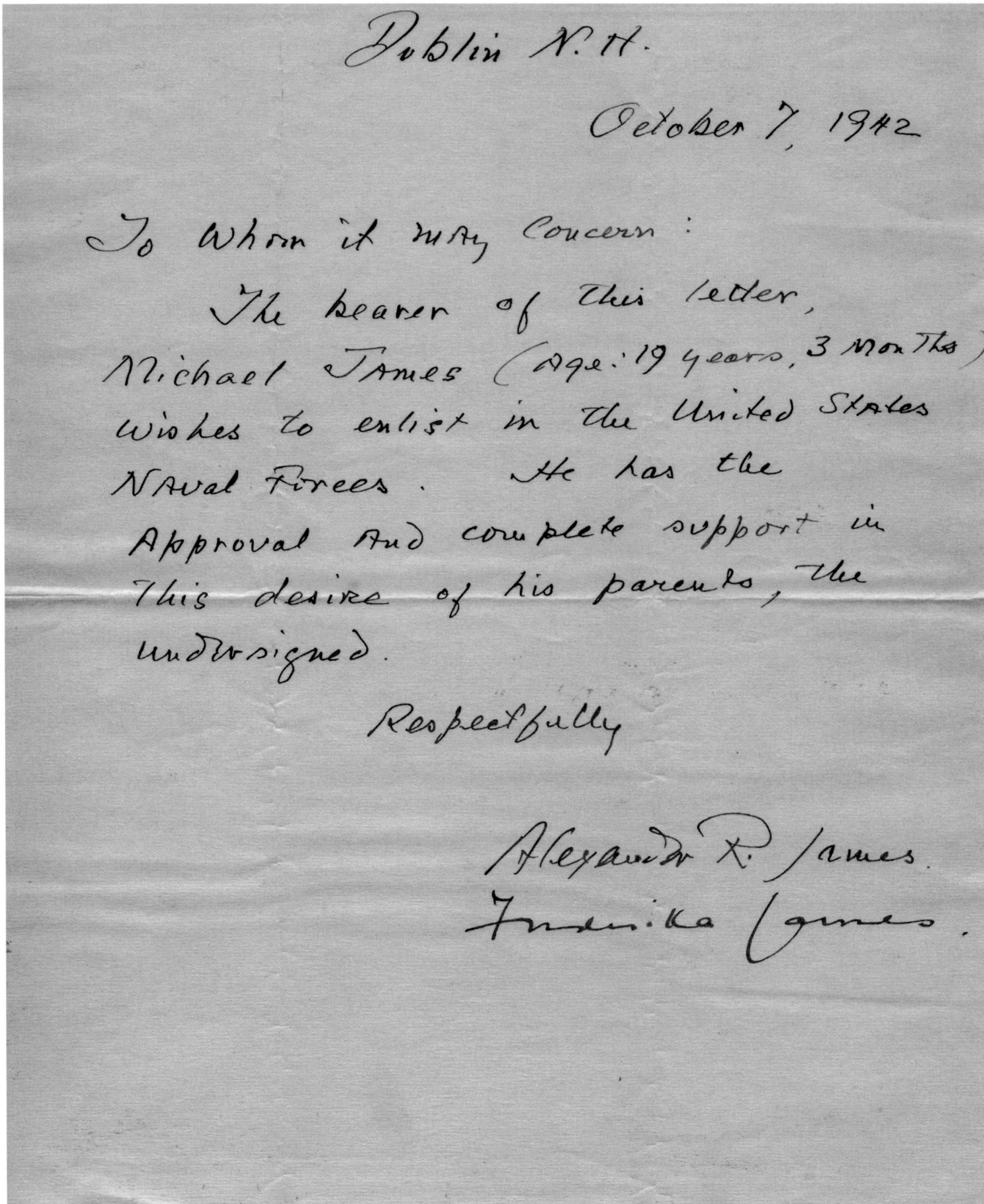

Dublin N.H.

October 7, 1942

To Whom it May Concern:

The bearer of this letter, Michael James (Age: 19 years, 3 months), wishes to enlist in the United States Naval Forces. He has the approval and complete support in this desire of his parents, the undersigned.

Respectfully

Alexander R. James.
Frederika James.

Letter from my parents to the U.S. Navy Recruiting Station in Boston.

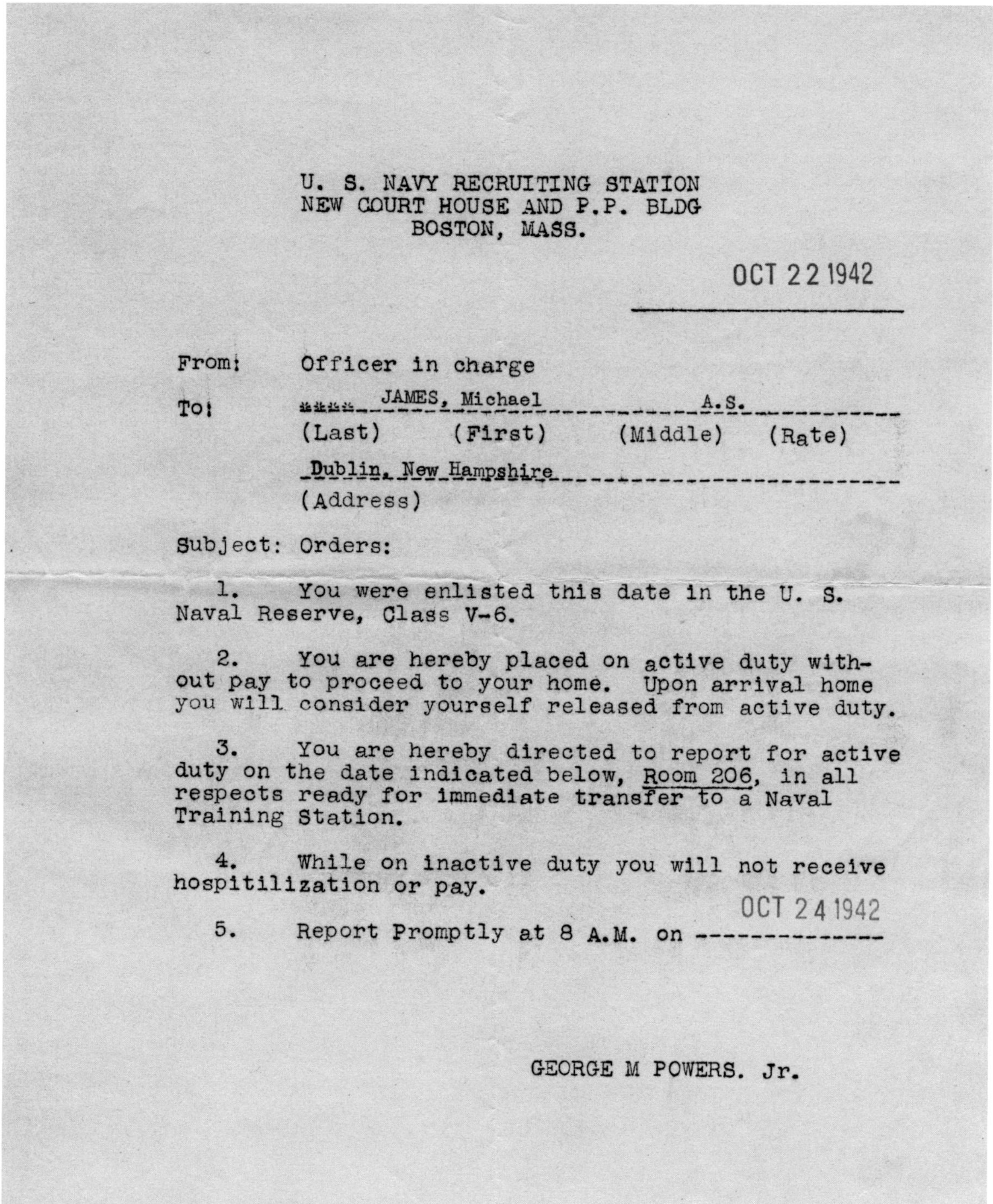

U. S. NAVY RECRUITING STATION
NEW COURT HOUSE AND P.P. BLDG
BOSTON, MASS.

OCT 22 1942

From: Officer in charge

To: JAMES, Michael A.S.
(Last) (First) (Middle) (Rate)

Dublin, New Hampshire
(Address)

Subject: Orders:

1. You were enlisted this date in the U. S. Naval Reserve, Class V-6.

2. You are hereby placed on active duty without pay to proceed to your home. Upon arrival home you will consider yourself released from active duty.

3. You are hereby directed to report for active duty on the date indicated below, Room 206, in all respects ready for immediate transfer to a Naval Training Station.

4. While on inactive duty you will not receive hospitilization or pay.

5. Report Promptly at 8 A.M. on OCT 24 1942

GEORGE M POWERS. Jr.

My enlistment orders.

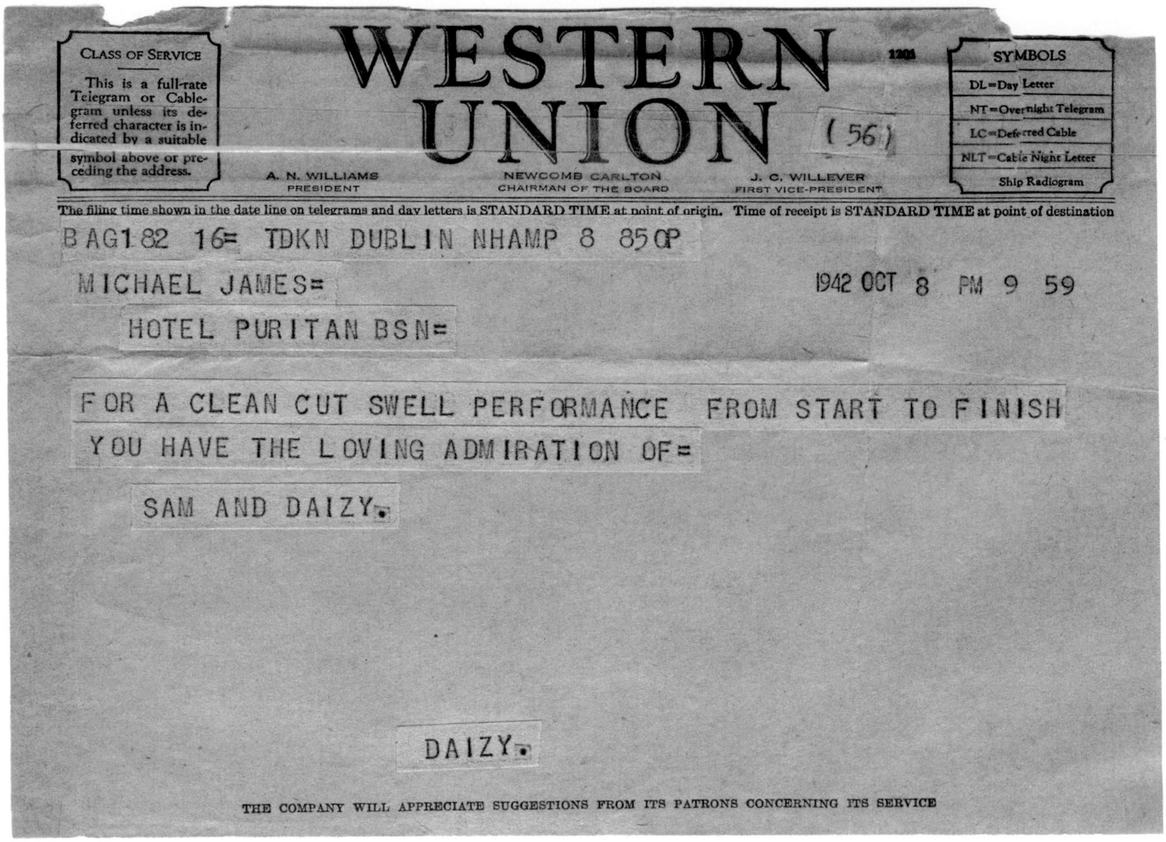

CLASS OF SERVICE

This is a full-rate Telegram or Cablegram unless its deferred character is indicated by a suitable symbol above or preceding the address.

WESTERN UNION

(56)

A. N. WILLIAMS, PRESIDENT — NEWCOMB CARLTON, CHAIRMAN OF THE BOARD — J. C. WILLEVER, FIRST VICE-PRESIDENT

SYMBOLS

DL=Day Letter
NT=Overnight Telegram
LC=Deferred Cable
NLT=Cable Night Letter
Ship Radiogram

The filing time shown in the date line on telegrams and day letters is STANDARD TIME at point of origin. Time of receipt is STANDARD TIME at point of destination

BAG182 16= TDKN DUBLIN NHAMP 8 850P

MICHAEL JAMES= 1942 OCT 8 PM 9 59

HOTEL PURITAN BSN=

FOR A CLEAN CUT SWELL PERFORMANCE FROM START TO FINISH YOU HAVE THE LOVING ADMIRATION OF=

SAM AND DAIZY.

DAIZY.

THE COMPANY WILL APPRECIATE SUGGESTIONS FROM ITS PATRONS CONCERNING ITS SERVICE

Telegram from my parents following my induction into the Navy. (To add humor, my father used pen names Sam and Daizy, a batty couple from up the street.)

The Adventures of M. James

Me.

[Gerald R. Ford Library]

FIRST CRUISE

September 15, 1943 to January 22, 1945

September 15 From U.S. Naval Air Station, Cape May, N.J. (had been there for several months following bootcamp in Newport, Rhode Island), I reported aboard the USS *Monterey,* aircraft carrier, CVL-26. It was late afternoon and I went into Philly for supper with shipmates Jim and Jean. Returned at midnight and had one hell of a time finding my sack, below three others, which is in forward end of the ship. They call it the bow. Turns out it was aft. Also, the bunk is on fourth deck below, and I was on third. Finally oriented, I threw up, and spent rest of night thinking about it all. Never did find the bunk. Lots of empties, though, and lots of noise, too. Farts, chatter, snoring, and air pumps.

September 16 Spent most of day checking in. Right now, the *Monterey* is living up to the tradition that a ship is clean at sea, dirty in port. She's a mess. In afternoon, went into Philly to call Dublin[1] and was told that Sandy's having a tough time finding himself a job, and that Danny seems better. Wrote letters in YMCA, returning to ship at midnight. Came aboard with cuffs rolled up. Got hell. Also, on gangplank, forgot to salute a flag that wasn't there. Hell, again. A poor night, and many more like them there'll be until I get used to having my head stepped on (there're three bunks above mine), until I get used to a ventilator that blows dock air into my

(opposite) USS *Monterey* under way for battle in the Pacific.

1. My hometown of Dublin, New Hampshire.

face, until I get accustomed to the squawkbox that sounds bugles and whistles all night long, and until I learn to sleep with a ship on fire. A welder incinerated a room full of stowed bunks, and it took nearly four hours to get the thing out. None of the above contributes to good sleeping. There's nothing about this place remotely like home.

September 17 Skipped chow this morning. They're loading on ammunition today, and cleaning up the ship. We're soon to pull out. Can't say I've enjoyed myself here. Better the seas than this shipyard. Am resigned to anything, though the head is one hell of a place, no more than an open trough where one and all rub elbows now and then. Impossible to relax. Still not easy to find my way around. Will try to get ashore tonight.

September 18 On liberty, read *Time* in an Italian restaurant, returning to ship by midnight, where they were loading on planes. Will soon be shoving off. Food remains poor, and with worse to come. Already, worms in the bread. Am not complaining, though; just getting off my chest what I can't get into the stomach.

September 19 At noon, hitched into New York where I saw the H.J.s,[1] and had a good time. Got back by 1 AM. Am told we're going to Brazil, then on to Hawaii and New Caledonia, wherever that is.

September 20 This morning was told to get ready to shove off. Up anchored around noon. Saw Cape May at a distance, and she was good to see—at a distance. Am forever reminding myself that I *wanted* all this. Smooth seas, and no upchucking yet.

September 21 Calm sea. Moving at 10 knots. No sickness yet. This evening, first of twice-daily battlestations. Whistles and bugles and much alarm. At first, thought ship may have been sinking. Got out of Chesapeake Bay alive.

---

1. My Uncle Harry and his wife, Dorothea.

Loading ship at Philadelphia Naval Yard.

[Gerald R. Ford Library]

September 22 Midwatch (in aerological office immediately below flight deck, forward), and upchucked most of the time, portside. Had lots of company. By evening, were a few miles off Florida. Flying fish. Got hell tonight for penetrating the chartroom for a weather map demanded by the bridge. Was actually yelled at by the Executive Officer. A mean man. A nervous one, too. I had the impression they were lost. Officers relieve themselves on the enlisted men. Will begin a beard in the morning.

September 23 Off San Salvadore this PM. Gave Columbus a thought. Man wringing out a swab fell overboard. One of the two destroyers took him in. Temp is 95° in aero office. Waters blue as a Maxfield Parrish. In AM, stood in line for nearly two hours for chow. Some joke: a 9:30 breakfast in a war. Will be issued a life preserver today which must be worn at all times. Have not yet given thought to a drowning. Mountbatten: "Funny how one feels he'll survive himself." We're heading for the Panama Canal they say. Makes sense. My sack is in a cubbyhole where

Francis E. White became a lifelong friend who later named his son Michael James.

laundry is stowed. Hot. If bombed at night, the enemy would do well to know that there's a gas chamber on my right, an ammunition dump at my feet, and the boiler room's below. New aerographer, White, aboard. He's ten years my senior. At long last I've someone to talk to. A good mind, and a good sense of humor, too. Tried to have him moved from stern to forward quarters, but was told, "We can't risk losing all you aerographers." Even the stewards are scattered. Have yet to catch a sight of the Captain.

September 25 Went through Panama Canal, an 8-hour run. Liberty that very night, and went into the city with aerology crew. Got tight on gin rickies. Whores. Thousands of soldiers and sailors all over the place. Sent ten postcards to Dublin. The town's like a carnival, though not a happy one. Had a good time. Returned to ship in time for the AM watch.

September 26 Moved bunk today, and will now be sleeping in an aft quarters, less fashionable, they say, but safer. The bow's a dangerous berth. This ship is given a year at most. The movie, *My Son, My Son,* was flashed on the flight deck bridge. Still in Panama. Soon heading for San Diego.

September 27 Pulled out at 0810 this morning, and followed a coastline all day long. Some beautiful mountains, though. Though tired, am feeling on crest of the wave. Never enough sleep. Fair food. Absolutely no privacy. Am on a top bunk now. Better air. Foul air rises, though. I don't understand it.

September 28 Surrounded by water. That's about it. As am writing this on the 30th, am able to say that around midnight of the 28th, there'll

Monterey at sea.

be an exchange of fire between the two destroyers and a sub. Heard the shots. No word on results. Am planning to eat but two meals a day because of those endless lines. Worse than Washington. Terribly hot down there in the sleeping quarters. Mustache taking shape. Have given up on the motheaten beard. Have been told that the next leave will be a "Survivor's Leave." Am looking forward to that with surprising good cheer. Maybe within six months. Very easy to land on "report" aboard this ship.

September 30 Constipated, and with no relief in sight. The heads are so disagreeable that any sign of possible action disappears the moment of entry. Maybe in October. A hurricane may be brewing. That should relieve the monotony. Everyone beefs all day long. Patriotism is a laugh. Have yet to feel really angry at the Japs. Hitler I fear and despise.

October 1 Nothing much today. Hot. Though am drinking all day long (de-salted water), I never seem to pee. Had a crap, though. It could have sunk the Japanese navy. Spent two hours talking and arguing about socialism and religion with AerM 1/c Fassbinder,[1]

1. Aerographer's Mate first class, Fassbinder was later killed.

and with striker Long. A real good airing. Long was kicked out of N.Y.U. during the Bertram Russell mess.

October 3 Pay day. Forty dollars. Arrived San Diego all foggy and cool. We're taking off planes, replacing them with smaller ones. Army fighter types. F6F's, or whatever. Liberty. Spent the night trying to find Sandy, who doesn't live at his address.

October 5 Pulled out in PM. Fifteen hundred additional sailors are aboard (guests) who alone more than equal our overcrowded complement of 1330. Jesus, it'll be a mess. Believe we're heading for Pearl Harbor, a five-day trip. Every man on ship has been designated a "buddy" to look after. Mine is one Jacobs, a real dullard. Gave him my sack for duration of ride, a real big gesture on my part. No reaction. Dull. In the meantime, I'll be sleeping on the balloonroom floor. Cold metal. Two meals a day for all hands. No showers.

October 6 Spent a long night on the flight deck, cold as hell, but better than the floor. My "buddy" Jacobs, he complains it's crowded down there. Tough. We'll be unloading him in Hawaii. Am finding humor in nearly everything.

October 8 Am pooped. No sleep. Haven't seen bunk since Diego. Quante and I, equals in rate, have been told we're going to move into the balloonroom where the helium tanks are stowed.[1] Sleeps four. Big improvement. It's immediately below the flight deck, opening on to a gunmount. Nights will be cooler. Quante's from New Mexico.

October 9 In PM, pulled into Pearl. It was nearly two years ago while taking a shower at Pomfret School, and following a hike with the Joseph Barrells,[2] that I learned of the strike on Pearl Harbor. Thought the harbor was somewhere off Maine. Little did I think I'd soon be there. Saw same wreckage. Danny's on my mind. All

1. Helium for the weather balloons.
2. Joe was my English teacher.

passengers are off. Wake Island's been bombed by five or six carriers. Needless to say, the *Monterey* was not among them. Talked to some guys who were on the raid. Twenty-six planes were lost, most of them having run out of gas. A plane with no tail landed on the carrier *Cowpens*, burning up most of the gun crew. We're to consider Wake a practice run. Nine carriers are now in port, waiting around for the business.

News of the sinking of Danny's ship in 1941. He went on to serve in the Field Service in Burma.

Ship Sunk Off Hawaii

WAILUKU, Maui, Hawaii, Dec. 22 (Delayed) (U.P.)—Thirty survivors of the Matson freighter Lahaina, shelled and sunk by a Japanese submarine, were reported weak but otherwise in good condition today after drifting, rowing and sailing for ten days through heavy winds and waves.

They beached their lifeboat at Spreckelsville, Maui, at daybreak Sunday, after a hazardous and painful voyage negotiated safely under the command of Captain H. O. Matthiesen. Four crew members were killed in the attack.

The Maui medical disaster committee under the direction of Colonel C. B. Lyman was on the job a few minutes after the beaching of the lifeboat. It sped the survivors to the Puunene Hospital, where the district surgeon, Major C. J. Cranston, pronounced them fit, but for exhaustion.

Survivors said the submarine fired twenty-five rounds at the Lahaina, scoring twelve hits, but used no torpedoes. They said it fired continuously as it advanced from a range of 2,000 yards.

The crew abandoned ship but remained in the vicinity until the following morning, when Captain Matthiesen reboarded the Lahaina and retrieved apples, lemons and carrots, which he issued sparingly, along with the limited water supply. The water ran out entirely on Saturday.

Soon after the captain left the ship with the food, it sank, and the lifeboat headed for Maui through a westerly wind and heavy waves.

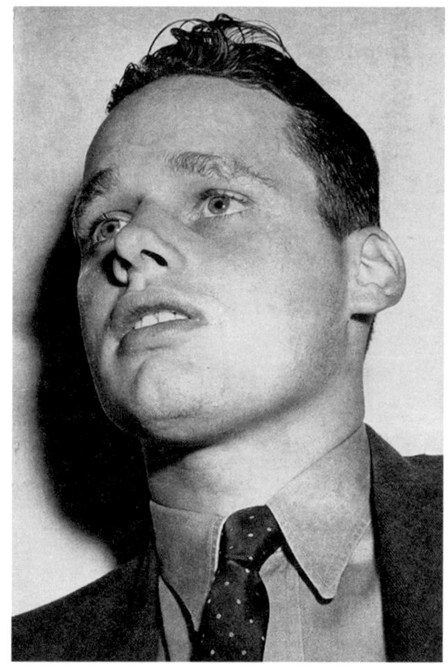

Danny.

The crew members were loud in their praise of Captain Matthiesen, agreeing that his skillful navigation and philosophical handling of the men saved their lives.

One, an American of Japanese ancestry, was called by his mates "a real American." A Hawaiian, Henry J. Fern, performed heroically at oar and sail and was particularly valuable in helping ride out the mountainous waves encountered at times.

The attack was denounced as piratical and cowardly. Although a warning shot was fired, the men said, the firing continued without a moment's pause until the mortal blow had been dealt to the ship.

October 11 Liberty at 9 AM. Hopped a bus for Waikiki, where striker Rachlin and I went swimming in beautiful blue-green waters. Had a $3.00 steak. Went to a whorehouse on Congress Street. A little "blackass Kanaka" in pink bib kept saying, "Two minute, two minute." Couldn't perform. No one got more than two minutes. Humiliating. Went shopping. Got a sweatshirt, money-belt, a record book, and some postcards. Hope to find Dad a ball of string.

October 15 During General Quarters (a test drill), ran up a ladder whose hatch had already been secured (was late for my post), sinking brains into a steel nobbin. Much bleeding. Eight stitches. First blood.

MJ, Waikiki.

Dave Payton, Tink Candy (friend from boot camp), and MJ, Waikiki.

October 19 Long, my socialist friend, transferred to shore duty. Will miss the good talk. There's a rumor that this will be a flagship if that Admiral stays aboard. Unlikely. We're too small. This morning, moved to Pearl City where most of the carriers are.

October 24 That Admiral just now departed this ship, so that takes care of that, and a lucky thing, too. Discipline's already all too tight, and besides, as a flagship aerographer, lots more would have been expected of me. For instance, I still can't operate the rasonde[1] machine. Mathematics are involved, and calculus, too. Never passed algebra, even. Would have had to fake some of the readings. Lately, we've been on maneuvers some two hundred miles out of Hawaii. Fair results. The Admiral said we'd better get better, though, at least before action. Am now sleeping in the balloonroom. Must not keep a diary. It's against navy regs, so says Adm. McCain. We'll see. During inspections I can hide it in the little safe where the weather codes are kept. That box is never opened for inspection. Weatherly's pint of gin is in there now.

October 27 Having returned to Honolulu for a couple of days, we're now off for more maneuvers. Already, a sub's been sighted. It was a mile off, though, and we missed it. I see what the Admiral meant.

1. Short for radiosonde, an instrament that radios back atmospheric measurements from helium balloons.

[Gerald R. Ford Library]

Loading bombs.

[US Navy]

F6F Hellcat fighter coming up from hangar deck on elevator.

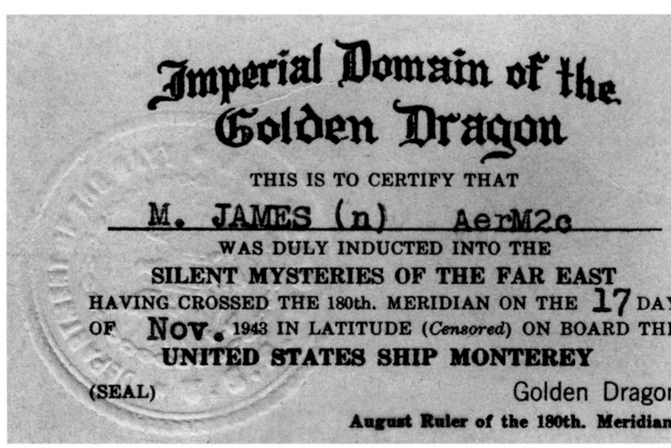

Imperial Domain of the Golden Dragon

THIS IS TO CERTIFY THAT

M. JAMES (n) AerM2c

WAS DULY INDUCTED INTO THE

SILENT MYSTERIES OF THE FAR EAST

HAVING CROSSED THE 180th. MERIDIAN ON THE 17 DAY OF Nov. 1943 IN LATITUDE (*Censored*) ON BOARD THE

UNITED STATES SHIP MONTEREY

(SEAL) Golden Dragon

August Ruler of the 180th. Meridian.

Certificate issued when crossing the 8th meridian (International Date Line) for the first time.

October 30 Back here at Pearl for few days.

November 3 Practice invasion of the Hawaiian Islands. Three days of it. A plane catapulted into the sea at 4 AM. Pilot picked up eight hours later. Three carriers are with us, among them the new, improved *Lexington*, and six destroyers.

November 10 Departed Pearl as one of two task groups. We're composed of 4 carriers, 8 destroyers, 3 cruisers, 1 battlewagon, and some tankers. The forward group is the bigger one. The Captain says we're headed for the Gilbert Islands. Troop ships are in the forward force. Poor food. Worms in the flour. Little change in the crew's appearance, psychologically. Executive Officer announced this morning (now November 12th) that on Wednesday last, Rabaul was bombed by yet another force. The Japs lost 3 ships and 58 planes. Our force lost 15 planes. Ten pilots are missing, and ten are wounded. Near hits on carriers. This could be a diverting war, after all.

November 19 General Quarters at 0300. Got up at two. Bombed Makin all day. Constant GQ. Horrible sandwiches, spam between shingles. No planes attacked us, but we did lose a plane over the side. Pilot rescued. Meager anti-aircraft from the island. The Japanese seem to have a lack of planes. We're ten miles off.

November 20 Mum's birthday. Would give her Makin if I could. Bombed it all day. Better yet, troops landed. No opposition. Got a sight of the island in PM. It's flat. All the Japs were killed. We'll circle it for a week while an airfield's being built.

November 21 General Alarm at 0300. It's now 10 minutes later, and bogies[1] are approaching. One was just now shot down in sight of us. The other one's turning back. My battle station is here in the office. I'll not know much of the war *this* way. Will try to have it returned to balloonroom. If one's in a war, he might as well see it.

1. An unidentified (usaully enemy) aircraft.

[Gerald R. Ford Library]

F6F about to take off.

November 25 Thanksgiving, and all the trimmings. Fine meal. Makin's been taken, and Tarawa, too. Yesterday, one of our Kaiser carriers was sunk (*Monterey* class), and with tremendous loss. Burned in sight of us. Sobering. This evening, the Japs dropped flares all around us. A beautiful sight, really. Little fires floating in the sky. One plane was shot down. No bombs were dropped. Am back in the balloonroom for GQs. (The war may now continue!) Their mission was to photograph us, I guess. So as not to reveal their positions, carriers are not supposed to fire at night. (If a kamikazi is obviously zeroing in, I imagine we might.) I feel strangely disappointed when approaching planes have no intention to bomb us. The carrier *Independence* has been torpedoed, and is now off to Figi for repairs. Should soon be leaving this

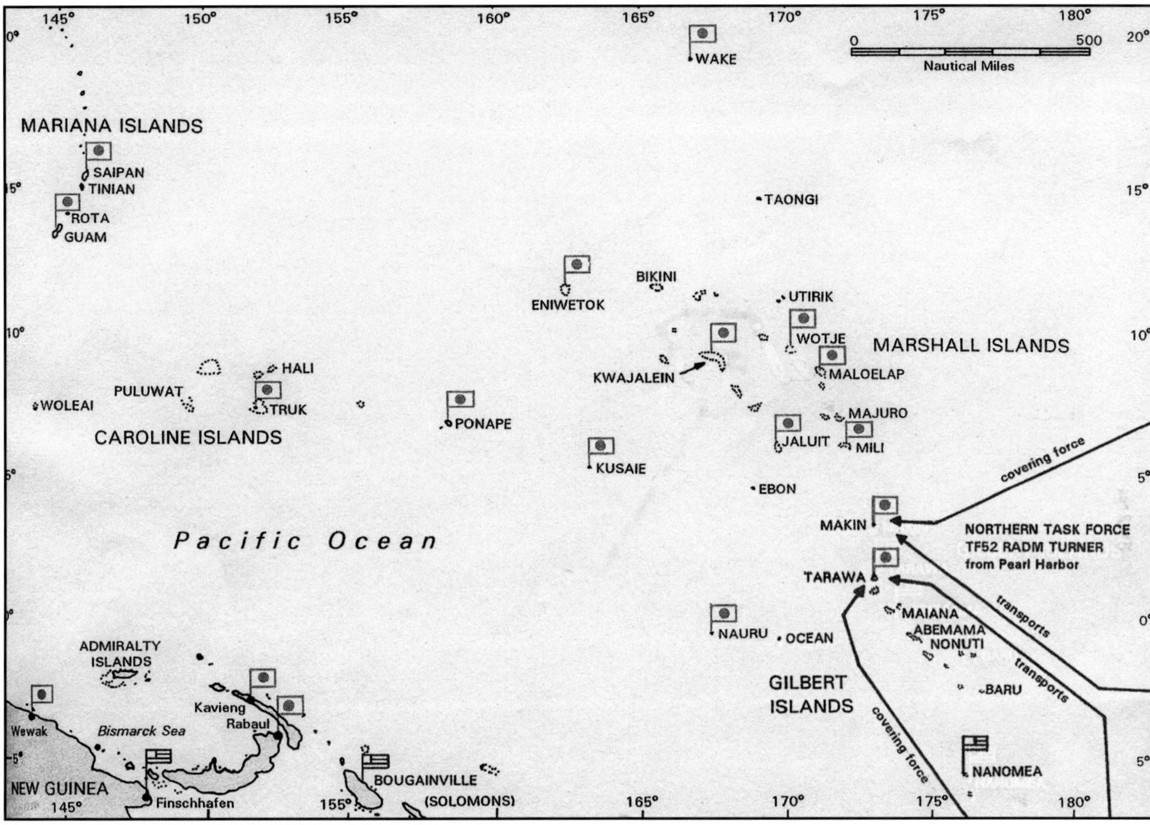

Assault on Gilbert Islands, November 1943.

[William E. Terheun collection]

area for the Marshalls. (Made AerM 2/c three weeks ago.) Am growing fond of sea duty, as opposed to the *idea* of it, which was the case at Cape May. Of course, I'm a pacifist at heart. Am getting others interested in drawing. Nudes, mostly. Joe Barrell has sent me *American Stories* and *Poetry*. Big success.

November 26 This evening, from 8 to 10, we had our third night attack, only a lot bigger than the others. One plane went right over the fantail, dropping a torpedo that missed us by inches. With luck like that, we'll never get back to the States. Other planes went overhead, but did no damage. Only if we're hit is there a chance for home. Was standing on the flight deck looking at the battleships and cruisers firing at the Japs, when all of a sudden I saw

[US Navy]

[US Navy]

Enemy planes plunge to the sea in flames.

[US Navy]

Diving for cover (and cheering) as tracer-bullets come in and a Japanese plane is shot down.

tracer-bullets spitting over my head. At the time, thought them from one of our ships, but as they came closer, realized we were being machine-gunned. Nearly shat. Fell to the deck. All over the flight deck men were scrambling for better positions to cover themselves, though some of them for better observation posts. A uniquely American scene, I was thinking. Shot down 7/7 Zeros,[1] or other types. It doesn't matter. We lost Lt. Comdr. O'Hara, who was decorated by F.D.R. last year.

November 29 Last night, the Japs came in again. Always at the same time. We left our convoy during the day to join another one. With us now are three battleships, six destroyers, and the *Bunker Hill*. We shot down two Japs, beautiful balls of fire falling to the sea. On flight deck it was like a football game, spectators surging from port to starboard for more favorable views of the action. Oil burned in water for long time. It seems that no one ever gives the pilot a thought, whether he may be dead or alive. I thought we were obliged to by terms of the Geneva Convention. Have been swinging a psychrometer on flight deck—under tracer bullets. They'll be back tonight. I have it good, though. Poor Sandy.

December 4 GQ sounded during movie. Five groups approached, but we went on to bomb Tarawa.

December 8 Up at 0300. Are on our way to the New Hebrides, our having left patrol of Makin under Nimitz for S.W. Pacific under Halsey. We bombed the hell out of Lauru Island. One of our planes had to land in water. Couldn't get its tailhook down. Went right over the bow. Pilot and two crew members rescued. The other carrier lost two planes. A destroyer lost 27 men when hit by shore fire. Have crossed the Equator without undergoing that "shellback" initiation. Too busy. It'll come later. Old salts can make it really rough on the virgins. The New Hebrides area will be lots hotter than the Central Pacific. Am practicing for a Christmas skit.

---

1. Japanese fighter planes.

Sunbathing.

[Gerald R. Ford Library]

Swimming off the bow.

December 10 Sandy's birthday. No word of Danny. No action, either.

December 12 Have pulled into Espiritu Santo, New Hebrides. Quite a simple piece of land. Liberty consists of cocoanut hunts. Nothing else to eat. Don't think we'll be here too long. Mail from Danny, Mum, and Betsy Lefferts.[1] She'll send me H.H. Munro's *Stories of Saki*.

December 15 Liberty! Every man got three chits (tickets), either for beer or for ice cream. Terrible beer. Island full of cocoanuts and abandoned plantations. Good swimming. A whaleboat turned over, and sixty drowned. Saw a tennis court! Forest Hills! Knives taken away from us.

December 22 Dad's birthday. Special orders to pull out. Left early this morning, though promised we'd be here for Christmas. Am thinking

1. Headmaster's wife at Pomfret School.

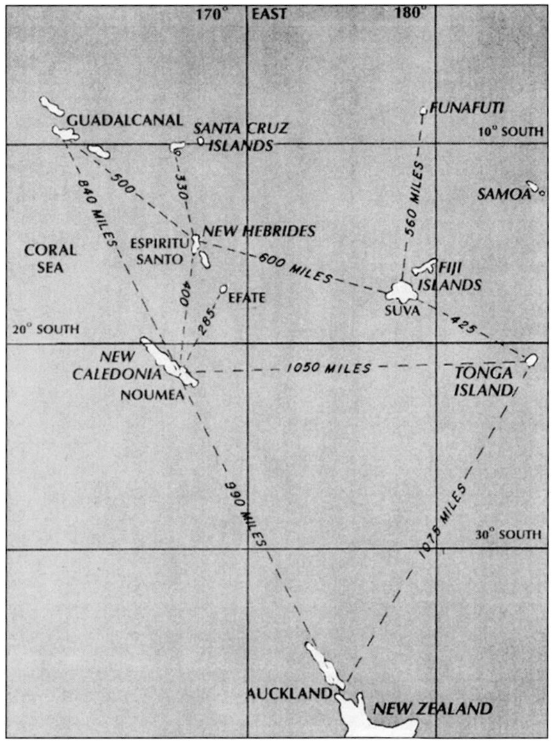

Espiritu Santo, New Hebrides.

[U.S. Government Printing Office]

those Special Orders say we're to intercept the Jap fleet at Rabaul. Should be interesting. Going 26 knots.

December 25 Up this morning at 0300, and planes off by 5 to raid Kavieng Harbor, New Ireland. Lost no planes. That's an important harbor right now. Sunk two freighters. Lost plane and pilot in PM, circling ship for a landing. Were attacked by 20-30 planes in evening. We shot down a Betty[1]—our first kill! It was an easy shot, though. Flew right over the ship. Later that evening, downed two more. Sometimes I wish I were less of a pacifist. It kills half the fun.

December 29 Were heading back to port when orders came to intercept a Jap convoy of battleships, cruisers, destroyers, and transports. It's south of Truk Island. We got as far as 3 degrees south, or about 300 miles opposite Rabaul, when orders came to turn back. Don't know why. Disappointed. Destroyers were fueled this morning.

1. Allied code name for Japanese patrol bomber plane with crew capacity of seven.

[US Navy]

Rough landing.

Damaged plane dumped overboard.

1944

January 1 Welcomed in the new year with an attack on Kavieng. Two of our pilots were shot down in a dogfight. Intense opposition. Two of our planes crash-landed on the deck. Had to be pushed overboard. Major damage was no more than bent propellers, but as other planes had to land, there was no time to fool around with them. $125,000 each. F6Fs they were. Pilots returned with wounds on scalps and legs. Lots of blood. Glad I'm not in the army. They hit a cruiser and two destroyers. No doubt we'll be attacked this evening. We struck at that task force as it was steaming toward

[US Navy]

Crew hurries to remove damaged plane from flight deck. (Arrow at right points to me.)

New Britain to relieve their men. We were outnumbered by 30 or more Zeros. In dogfight, we lost four planes and two pilots. The *Bunker Hill* lost four planes and four pilots. This evening, the Japs came within five miles of us, but it was thunderstorming, and they had to turn back. Disappointed.

January 2 In the middle of the night we turned around, for rather than heading for Espiritu Santo, orders were received to return to Kavieng where there were ships in the harbor. Did so, and sunk a couple of cruisers. Damaged a destroyer. In afternoon, four of our fighters intercepted five approaching Zeros, and downed them all. For the day, we lost no pilots, no planes.

January 5 Now on way back to E.S., but again, as twice in the past, more ships may be spotted in Kavieng, in which case we'll return to that theatre.

January 7 Pulled into Espiritu Santo today after a really quite agreeable sixteen-day outing. Expecting to be here a few days, no more.

January 10 Put on show. Did my Patrick Henry speech, plus impersonations of F.D.R., Eleanor, Commander Gazze, etc. Also, a Scrooge act by Yeoman Witkins, which got booed.

January 11 The show was put on ashore today, minus the Witkins flop. Lots of music and solos, etc. An audience of four thousand.

January 20 Yesterday, pulled out of Espiritu Santo, and today into Funafuti of the Ellis Island group. It's a bunch of little low sandmats. Many ships in "harbor," and more arriving from Pearl. Eight battlewagons. Am pretty sure we'll be heading for the Marshalls. No liberty here.

January 22 Have left Funafuti for the Marshalls. We're one of *seven* task groups. Will list ships on another day. This will be no picnic.

ANNIVERSARY ANTICS

Lieutenant Redavid - Director
C. Tompkins, S1c - Master of Ceremonies

1 - The Jive Bombers	*P. Such, PM1c, C&R - Conductor* -	*Saxaphone*
	C. Maffey, AOM1c, V - O	*Saxaphone*
	P. Semiele, S1c, V - 3	*Saxaphone*
	D. Decotis, AMM3c, V - 1	*Saxaphone*
	C. Gogham, F2c, M	*Trumpet*
	M. Carr, S1c, 3rd.	*Trumpet*
	C. Simonian, FC3c, 6th.	*Trombone*
	F. Brown, AMM2c	*Guitar*
	H. Lewis, S1c, V - 1	*Drums*
2 - Monterey Swingtet	*P. Such, PM1c, CzR*	*Saxaphone*
	F. Browu, AMM2c V - 1	*Guitar*
	H. Lewis, S1c, V - 0	*Drums*
	J. Bozic, AMM3c, VF - 28	*Accordian*
3 - Solo	*W. Tompas, AMM3c, V - 1*	
4 - Impersonations	*M. James, Aero 2c, V - 3*	
5 - Solo	*C. Durham, Stm 3c, S*	
~~6 - Banjo Solo~~	~~*E. Brown, Amm2c, V - 1*~~	
7 - Monterey Glee Club	*L. Couture, PhM2c - Conductor*	

J. Cheney Ens.	*G. Archambeawlt S1c*
D. Galgano S2c	*J. Couzens Pfc*
O. Bannon Rdm 3c	*M. Gordon Amm 2c*
J. Camera S1c	*J. Prioletzi Amm 2c*
W. Chuck S1c	*P. Shannon Pfc*
J. Gessner S1c	*W. Coffey Aer 2c*
S. Acton AMM1c	*G. Guenther S1c*
F. Christian QM3c	*P. Venturella Phm 2c*
V. *Koslosky AOM1c*	*C. Urbany AOM2c*
G. Biannucci MM1c	*J. Skurda AMM2c*

8 - Bozic And His Accordain
9 - Solo *F. Alfano S1c, V - 1*
10 - Hepcats *H. Rucker Stm 2c and C. Durham Stm 2c*
11 - Songsters *A. Galineau AMM3c, V - 1* *W. Tompas AMM3c, V - 1*
P. Shannon Pfc USMC *J. Couzens Pfc USMC*
W. Marsh Pfc USMC *T. Kearney Pfc USMC*
12 - Double Trouble (Tap Dance) *R. S. and R. A. Allen, S1c, V - 1*
13 - National Anthem

Program for anniversary show celebrating the day the keel of *Monterey* was laid down, December 29, 1941.

January 24 One of our planes ran out of gas today, plunging but a few hundred feet from the ship. The radioman didn't manage to get out. Pilot OK, picked up by a destroyer. A mere five minutes before the crash, word had been received by Airplot that they were running low on gas. Surely, they could have been waved aboard. Maybe not. Who knows? Anyway, the guy is dead.

Show's cast (MJ in front row, 4th from left).

Ship's band practicing in elevator shaft.

January 25 The ships in our task group are as follows: three carriers (*Bunker Hill*, *Cowpens*, *Monterey*), two battleships (*Iowa* and *New Jersey*—both recently commissioned, still green), the cruiser, *Wichita*, and ten destroyers. The battleships have left us to join other groups. As I said, there'll be seven groups in all. If they've a common purpose, no one's enlightened me. Jan. the 31st will be "dogday," I believe, the day the Marines and Army land. In meantime, we'll make a few strikes. There are two or three Marine armies, as well as regular army contingents. I guess the Common Purpose is to capture the Marshalls, though why *seven* task groups? Seems excessive. It won't be easy, I guess, as the Marshalls have been held for now over twenty-five years. The loss of a thousand men at Tarawa should be a lesson to us all, or leastwise to the generals. Captain Hundt is sick. Cat fever, they say. Yesterday, that destroyer that picked up our pilot (his gunner survived, too), came alongside, and we pulled them aboard on a cable. They were in sacks.

January 29 Today, rose at 3 AM, ate shit-on-the-shingle, and launched planes for attack on Kwajalein Island. Lost one plane. Picked up its crew. Not much opposition. Destroyed fifteen planes on the ground. GQ all morning. Condition "Easy" in PM. No attack at night, though bogies, one at a time, did approach us, no doubt to report size and location.

January 30 Attacked Eniwetok Island. That's funny—thought it'd be Kwajalein. Tomorrow, the troops land. We just sunk four ships in the harbor, troop barges, and some fifteen planes were smashed on the ground. When one of our destroyers took off to pick up the crew of a downed plane, it ran into a convoy of four ships, and sunk them. Just like that. Anyway, so says the Admiral. Little air opposition, though lots of antiair ack-ack.[1] Was promoted to AerM 2/c the other day. Tough exam. Cheated. Had to.

February 1 Invasion of Marshalls proceeding. This is the quietest invasion I've ever known. Japanese air power seems to be crippled. We've not yet been attacked. All small islands are being taken; after them, the bigger ones. It's interesting to hear play-by-play

1. Ackack is antiair gunfire.

description of invasion from man on plane to tank on ground. "Move tanks to rear," he says, "and bring up flamethrowers to area 112. See if those Japs are dead, or just playing possum in #12. Battlewagon salvoes only 40 yards forward of our troops." Also, and later, "I think we've got Peninsula 22. It looks like the Marines are holding inspection!" Tough opposition on land. All this lack of air opposition is encouraging, we may be out of here sooner than the Admiral thinks. Lost one pilot and three enlisted men. Two planes cracked up on landing, and were ditched overboard. One of them came in on its nose.

February 3 Still no air opposition. We might just as well be off Nantucket. The shore fighting's tough, though, and we're going forward. Went to dentist today. Big cavity.

February 4 This morning, pulled into Majuro, an atoll of the Marshalls. By nighttime, the other two task groups joined us, making this the biggest assembly of warships since Creation. Tremendous power. Doesn't make me feel too safe, though. The list of ships is as follows:

> Aircraft Carriers: *Enterprise*, *Essex*, *Monterey*, *Belleau Wood*, *Cowpens*, *Bunker Hill*, *Yorktown*, *Cabot*, *Intrepid*, *Nassau*, *White Plains*, and the *Kalinin Bay*.
>
> Battle Ships: *Iowa*, *New Jersey*, *South Dakota*, *Alabama*, *Washington*, *Massachusetts*, *Indiana*, and the *North Carolina*.
>
> Cruisers: *Pensacola*, *Salt Lake City*, *Chester*, *Wichita*, *Oakland*, and the *San Diego*.
>
> Destroyers: 545, 588, 670, 538, 667, 582, 406, 644, 589, 581, 653, 564, 629, 651, 547, 250, 652, 447, 407, 536, 587, 668, and 537.
>
> Destroyer Escorts: Di 028, Di 259, Di 026, Di 262, Di 030, and the Di 264.

Part of Task Force 58 off Majuro, an atoll of the Marshall Islands. *Monterey* in foreground.

As for the task groups;

TG 58.1: *Yorktown*, *Enterprise*, *Belleau Wood*, *Massachusetts*, *Indiana*, *Washington*, plus cans and carriers.

TG 58.2: *Essex*, *Intrepid*, *Cabot*, *South Dakota*, *Alabama*, *North Carolina*, plus cruisers and cans.

TG 58.3: *Bunker Hill*, *New Jersey*, *Iowa*, *Wichita*, *Cowpens*, *Monterey*, plus cruisers and cans.

On patrol: *Langley* and *Saratoga*, plus the cruisers *Boston* and *Baltimore*.

Still others here and there and about.

We're here either to disassemble or return to Pearl Harbor for transfers and so forth. Then again, we might just keep plugging forward, possibly to Wake Island, and then on to the Carolinas, whose bay is the center of a volcano.

February 7 Have departed Majuro for patrol duty, returning on the 8th. It's a one-day rotation patrol. All quiet.

February 12 Along with two or three task groups, left Majuro this afternoon for a run to Truk. That's how I see it. We're the only force with battleships, six in all, and there ain't no more. We're to circle around at entrance of Truk while the other forces bomb the Jap fleet, forcing it out into the open, if possible. Not much fun for its sailors. Glad I don't know them. Their emperor must be feeling very low. We're composed of those six battlewagons, eleven destroyers, and the carriers *Cowpens* and *Bunker Hill.* This may turn into the two navies clashing, which is what we've been after for now over a year. Radarman Lindsay has quit his balloonroom bunk (gunners made too much noise), and F. White has grabbed his space. A welcomed change. The *Massachusetts* is with us. That means Renouf is here.[1]

February 16 We were within forty miles of Truk today, two of our forces going in for a strike. The *Monterey* remained behind, as patrol. Boring. Though the island was taken by surprise, there was some opposition. In the harbor, destroyers and cruisers were hit, plus many cargo ships. When four cruisers escaped from the harbor, a couple of battlewagons went after them, sinking all four. Very sad, but that's how a war gets won. Three of our planes were operational losses, no combat ones. I can't understand why a bigger fleet wasn't there, nor why so little opposition. After dark, one of our forces was attacked. We strike again tomorrow.

February 17 Lost a pilot this morning, saved the crew. Bum motor. Been striking all day, sinking a lot of cargo ships, a destroyer or two,

1. Renouf Russell was a friend from Dublin, New Hampshire.

After Marshall Islands, Task Force 58 attacked Truk, February 17, 1944.

[U.S. Government Printing Office]

and one carrier. Not much opposition, and little ackack. I can't understand it. Either they're bluffing, or they've pulled out. Or lost interest. As I could, too, if things don't pick up. It does look good for the future, though, and that's fine. Actually, am not at all sorry to see no fireworks, for its absence means we're that much nearer the end of this business. I guess we'll be landing troops on Truk within a month.

February 18 Yesterday, pulled out of the Truk area, and sooner than expected. Sooner than I expected, anyway. Means there was little more to do, I imagine. We're certainly not retreating, it can't be that. Evidently, they'd pulled out much of their shipping. Unfortunate. Otherwise, it might have been a grander smash. Today, spotted an empty raft. Learned later that seventeen Japs had been on it. Ordered to abandon the thing, they refused (who wouldn't?), and were then taken prisoner. The destroyer *Burns* has seven aboard from an earlier capture, having sunk a sub-chaser a few nights ago. Tomorrow, we strike Ponape, easternmost of the Caroline Islands.

February 19 At three this morning, general alarm sounded. Bogies within six miles. The destroyer *Izzard* nailed one of them. Beautiful sight. A particularly sad time to die, though, at three in the morning. The sky looked like New Year's eve, flames twisting down among the tracer bullets. It all happens so quickly, leaving but a pool of burning oil. What must the fish think of it all! Traua[1] says we take off in the morning for Saipan, below Guam, thirteen hundred miles from Tokyo. So much for Ponape.

February 22 Were attacked by bogies at one in the morning. Saw one lovely one come down in flames. Burned for a long time. Attacked Saipan and Guam the whole day through. Light opposition. We're still thirteen hundred miles from Japan. Nearest, by far, of any force yet. Results of those attacks on Truk and Saipan as follows: TRUK—Roughly 200 planes destroyed, in air and on ground. Thirty to forty merchant ships sunk. (I always think of Danny when a merchant ship is sunk.) Two destroyers sunk, two cruisers, too. SAIPAN—Two cargo ships sunk, and many barges. Five planes were shot down, and thirty were destroyed on the ground. OUR LOSSES—One night fighter, four fighters, and a TBF.[2]

February 23 Bogies approaching and we're having to get planes off in a hurry. Just now saw one of the *Bunker Hill*'s land in water. Splash. Pilot rescued. Later in day. One of our pilots was losing his oil, smoking from tail, etc., and was about to jump when he must have thought, "Oh what the hell," and landed safely on deck. Made it. The Exec. Officer, Crazy Gazze, hopped up on wing to check the oil, fell off, and crushed his foot. Good. Oh yes, on Saipan we also strafed a herd of cows. Seems unreasonable, at best.

February 26 Arrived Majuro.

March 4 Arrived Pearl City, Honolulu.

---

1. Commander K.F. Traua was the Meterological Officer.
2. Grumlin TBF Avenger and the TBM are bomber planes.

MJ, John Curtis and Dave Payton, Honolulu.

Payton, MJ and Curtis, Honolulu.

March 5 First liberty in long time. Honolulu no longer considered in war zone, so rather than one of four sections having liberty each day, it's now two sections at a time, port and starboard. No good. Too crowded. Pearl City's miles from town, and there're few buses around. When I finally squeezed on to one, a guy asked, "Where's this one going?" "I don't know," I answered, "I just got on." Everyone is pooped. Will rest up when combat resumes. (Shellback Initiation officers had their own party. Drunk. My Aero. Officer, Traua, acting-navigator at the time, was drunk at the wheel. Confined to quarters. Much bitterness among the old

[Gerald R. Ford Library]

Crew members crossing the equator for the first time undergo Shellback Initiation.

salts, as they feel the officers aren't really initiated. The real thing can cripple a guy.) It doesn't look as though the transfers are going to be made this trip. I see Nimitz is saying we're going to take Truk. So that may be next. For liberty, withdrew fifty dollars from my account, and bought dad a huge ball of string. Little mail is coming aboard. I miss the Japs.

March 15 Danny's birthday. Pulled out of Pearl today, and not all that unexpectedly, I'm thinking, as last night we were in a state of great excitement getting supplies aboard. Was up till midnight hauling in helium tanks. The ship was to be painted (camouflaged) like the *Bunker Hill.* No soap. Now on our way to Majuro. The carrier *Hornet* is with us, named after the sunken one from which Doolittle launched that attack on Tokyo. The carrier *Intrepid*, torpedoed in the Marshalls, failed to make it home, and is now resting in Honolulu. Following repairs, she'll make a second attempt. She lost quite a few men. Night before we pulled out, Quante was transferred to an amphibious unit. His absence won't be mourned. AerM 2/c Coffee, the only shipmate I've come to blows with,[1] will occupy Q's bunk in the balloonroom, along with White and me. Gunners made so much noise last night (chatter), we had to secure the door. Hot as hell.

March 20 Arrived Majuro at noon—for two or three days of leisure, then off for more game. An aerological striker, George someone, reported for duty this morning.

March 22 Now heading for Palau. That's the scuttlebutt, anyway. It's an island about two miles beyond Yap, which brings us close to the Philippines. From there, maybe down to Kavieng and Rabaul. Then to the States? Will be six weeks out, I guess.

March 28 Going to strike Palau pretty soon—for two days and after that, I don't know what. Lots of talk about going back to the States. Bogies around us most of the time now, for we're not far from New Guinea. Shot one down today. A second one came within a mile, and escaped. There may be trouble tonight. Subs pretty active. Am hearing a depth charge now and then. Why we've not been torpedoed yet, I'll never know. This PM, around chow time, one of the *Hornet*'s planes crashed into the sea as she was about to make a landing. All hands picked up. About five minutes later, after I made it to the flight deck, a plane landing on the *Bunker Hill* went over her side. It's always quite a sight. Could hear it, even. Pilot picked up. A minute or so later, the plane's depth charges went off. They shouldn't have. The shock could have killed the pilot who was in deep enough water already. He

1. Had a dispute with him over a toaster in the Aerology Office.

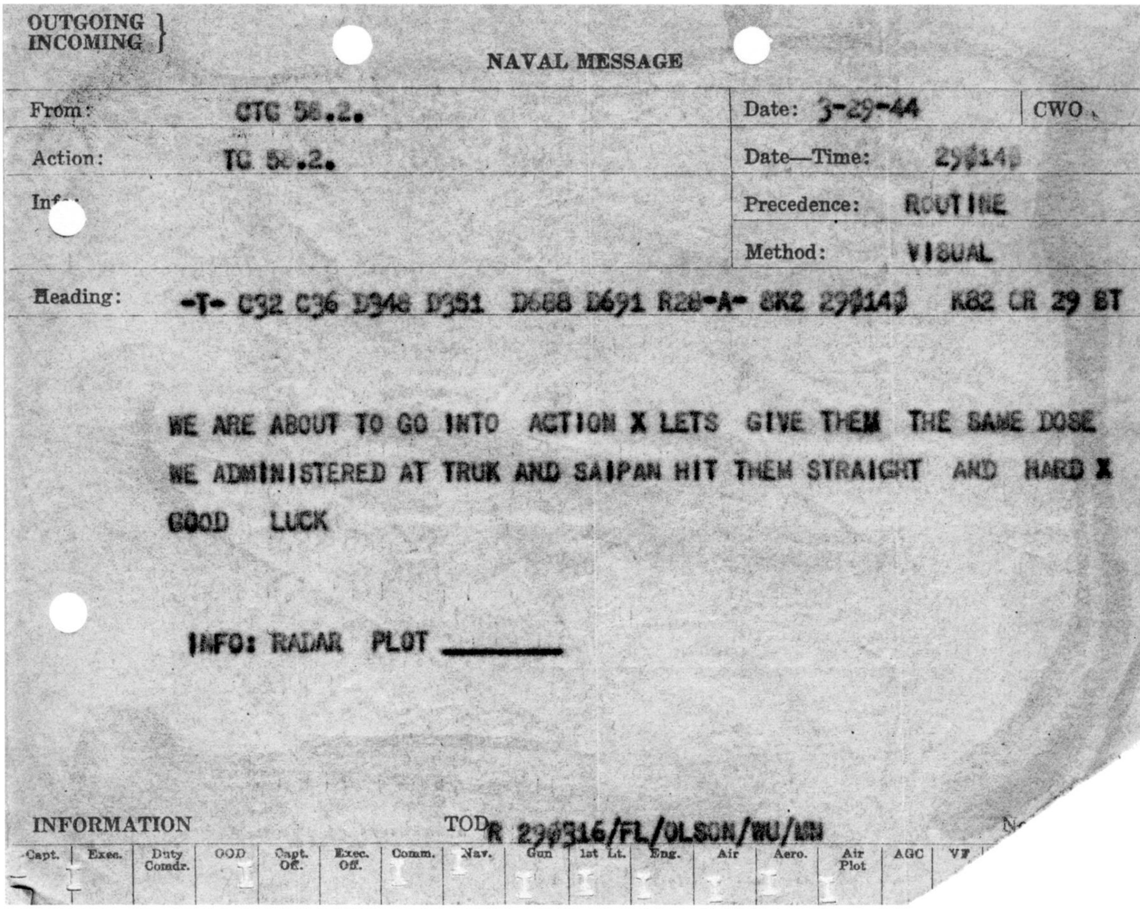

OUTGOING }
INCOMING }

NAVAL MESSAGE

From:	CTG 58.2.	Date:	3-29-44	CWO
Action:	TG 58.2.	Date—Time:	29Ø14	
Info:		Precedence:	ROUTINE	
		Method:	VISUAL	

Heading: -T- C32 C36 D348 D351 D688 D691 R28-A- 8K2 29Ø14Ø K82 CR 29 BT

WE ARE ABOUT TO GO INTO ACTION X LETS GIVE THEM THE SAME DOSE WE ADMINISTERED AT TRUK AND SAIPAN HIT THEM STRAIGHT AND HARD X GOOD LUCK

INFO: RADAR PLOT ______

INFORMATION TOD R 29Ø316/FL/OLSON/WU/MN

Capt.	Exec.	Duty Comdr.	OOD	Capt. Off.	Exec. Off.	Comm.	Nav.	Gun	1st Lt.	Eng.	Air	Aero.	Air Plot	AGC	VF

Rear Admiral A.E. Montgomery wishes us luck as we head for Palau.

wasn't below his neck, and that's what saved him. In our task group are four carriers, two battlewagons, six cruisers, and sixteen destroyers. In the other two groups are a total of seven cruisers, four battleships, eight carriers, thirty-two destroyers, three oilers, three Kaiser jobs, and six orphaned cans, a grand total of eighty-one ships. Man fell overboard after dark. Of course, the fleet couldn't stop. He'll swim around to a lonely death.

March 30 Raided Palau this morning, as we will all day, and tomorrow, too. Last night, we were attacked again. Shot down two. As always, it was quite a show, a lovely sight. Magnificent colors. Sorry for the

A downed pilot lucky enough to be picked up.

pilots. Several waves came in, wave after wave, hanging around no longer than an hour. None of our ships was hit. I don't get it. Surely the Japanese are better than that, and our gunners aren't perfect, either. A guy from some carrier tried to get too good a view of the show, and fell over the side. He, too, was left to drown as stopping to find him could mean the loss of some ships. Lots of subs around. In afternoon, two Japs were shot down about forty miles away. Don't yet know results of today's raids. All our planes from the first strike returned safely, some pretty badly shot up. In today's raid, twelve big cargo ships were sunk, and Palau was pretty well blasted. Some ackack, but little air opposition, interception. The island is surrounded by overlapping edges, which is bad news for our troops, should they have to land, invade, or whatever. Impossible, I'd say. Were attacked this evening (still on alert) and shot down fifteen, the fleet did. Because of a full moon, they used flares but twice. Didn't need them. Even so, none of our ships was hit. It was so bright, in fact, that we could easily see them. A four and a half hour raid. I must remember that they, too, have families. Sometimes I forget.

March 31 Early this morning, a can sunk a Jap cargo ship in sight of our forces. Will raid Palau again today. One task group has left us for a raid on Yap. Yesterday a pilot was shot down near Palau. Picked up by one of our subs. A second downed pilot was rescued by a seaplane from a battleship. As there was no room in the plane, he was tied to a wing! Saw two planes land in water. Operational losses. Crews saved. People look so small in the ocean. Last night, spent most of it on flight deck surging with the crowd, starboard to port, back and forth as the changing scene demanded. Lots of action. It would not have sounded unnatural had a voice cried out, "Peanuts, popcorn, and franks." Another guy fell overboard yesterday. Don't know if picked up. My recurrent nightmare is one in which I see my ship disappearing in the distance. Other times, I'm sliding down the flight deck toward the sea, never quite to splash. Right now, the Japs are flying in from the west. Will probably be intercepted before they hit us. This morning, over Palau, we shot down nineteen Zeros, destroying ten on the ground. All planes returned safely. This has been about the cleanest sweep yet. Pilots report the Japs were doing aerobatics without apparent purpose. At one time there were five parachutes coming down, one here, one there, all over the sky. One of our pilots didn't have the heart to shoot them down. Glad his friends didn't, either. We strike another island tomorrow. Yap will be hit by others. Planes intercepted.

April 1 No bogies last night, but we shot one down at sunrise this morning. Also, this morning, three cargo ships were sunk not fifteen miles distant. Attacked Woleai today, westernmost isle of the Truk Carolines. No results yet. Truk will get it in a couple of days. Tomorrow, we take on fuel.

April 2 On the 31st, *Monterey* pilots accounted for 25 of the 40 planes shot down that day. At two this morning, some poor guy from the *Wichita* fell overboard. It was raining, too. So solitary a death.

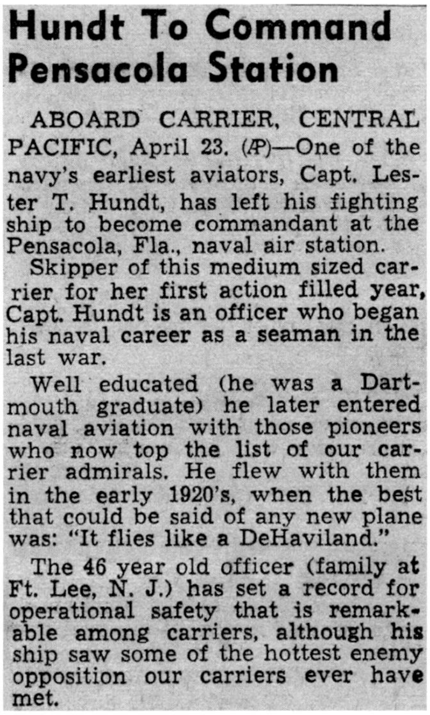
Hundt To Command Pensacola Station

ABOARD CARRIER, CENTRAL PACIFIC, April 23. (AP)—One of the navy's earliest aviators, Capt. Lester T. Hundt, has left his fighting ship to become commandant at the Pensacola, Fla., naval air station.

Skipper of this medium sized carrier for her first action filled year, Capt. Hundt is an officer who began his naval career as a seaman in the last war.

Well educated (he was a Dartmouth graduate) he later entered naval aviation with those pioneers who now top the list of our carrier admirals. He flew with them in the early 1920's, when the best that could be said of any new plane was: "It flies like a DeHaviland."

The 46 year old officer (family at Ft. Lee, N. J.) has set a record for operational safety that is remarkable among carriers, although his ship saw some of the hottest enemy opposition our carriers ever have met.

Capt. Hundt leaves *Monterey*.

Capt. Stuart H. Ingersoll, Hundt's replacement, on the bridge.

April 6 Arrived Majuro. Loading on stores. Guess we're going to New Guinea. The Captain's making Commodore. What a laugh. He should be making Admiral. Hate to see him leave. He's said goodbye.

April 10 The new Captain's about to come aboard. There'll be a new Exec., too (good riddance), and a new Aerological Officer, a full lieutenant. Will be sorry to see Traua go, a most fair man. I've been here too long, longer than anyone I know. Lots of talk about our going back to Pearl, or even to the States, ditching the raid on New Guinea. Urgent need for repairs. (Didn't know anything was broken.) Last night, bombs were removed. So that's it, I guess—Pearl or the States. Dear God that it be home. Fourteen carriers are here.

MJ looking for enemy subs.
(Maybe tomorrow.)

April 13 Pulled out of Majuro this morning—for New Guinea. Looks like home is out of the picture. Have been enlightened, and we *do* need urgent repairs. The carrier *Bataan* is now with us. Haven't figured out the new Captain yet. Traua is still acting-exec.

April 18 Rumor has it we're going to land 50,000 troops on New Guinea, against a Japanese estimate of 60. On the other hand, our concentrated attacks on such places as Hollandia would more than offset their superior numbers. We land on the 22nd, I think. At any rate, this is D-minus 4 day. Makes sense. I hear that after this attack, our force completes it's first chapter. That'd bring us to the 30th. We'd then return to base for further orders, for chapter two. I still think we'll be heading back to the States. The boilers are in need of urgent repair. Traua showed us a rusty pipe this evening, and said, "Here's our ticket to 'Frisco. I wouldn't use this in an outhouse." Right now, we're making contact with two enemy subs (they're lurking around) and bogies are on the screen. This morning, a floating mine was detected. Blasted, too. Last night, some poor guy fell overboard from a forward ship. We probably passed him. Drowned. We're never found at night.

It must be the sorriest of deaths, all alone, and the silence, his ship disappearing over the horizon. Nowhere to go but down. M.P.s never go topside after dark, not even the popular ones.

April 19 General Alarm before daybreak. We fired at some planes that turned out to be U.S. Army. They didn't have their IFFs turned on.[1] Inexcusable. It disrupted the sleep of thousands. Woke *them* up, too. Luckily, none of them was hit.

April 20 Carrier *Cowpens* shot down a Betty this morning, some twenty miles from us. From that distance, easily she could have seen the entire force, and radioed our position, even on her way down, maybe. We'll be attacking New Guinea (Hollandia) all day tomorrow. Spam sandwiches around the clock. Will invade N.G. the following day. More Spam. Rumor goes that after Hollandia, there'll be one more island, and then to the States. Beautiful. Shot down a Betty this afternoon. After that, the Captain gave a short speech. Said the plan's to strike with such might ("soften her up") that the army, the following day, could take whatever survivors by total surprise. Doubt that they'll fall for that. More bogies tonight, and same old stuff. Flares, etc. The *Bunker Hill* sent up nightfighters, first time since O'Hara was downed. We all need some time in the States. Though that's about all we think about, there's now talk of hitting the Philippines. The States or not, it looks like a long war. Glad I'm not in the army, though. Poor Sandy.

April 21 Here it is midnight, and not a Jap in sight. Amazing. Encouraging, too. Their airpower is definitely on the wane. Many planes destroyed at Hollandia, a few of them shot out of the air, but only a few. No losses for us. Saw a *Bunker Hill* plane catapult into the sea. Not three seconds later, a plane flew right over it, right on schedule. Sentimentality is not a pilot's major imperfection. Invasion tomorrow! As far as the Navy's concerned, this one looks like the easiest yet. We'll be patrolling for

1. Identification Friend or Foe, radar system.

a few days. Talk of our returning to the States has become more persistent. No results of raid yet.

April 23 Yesterday, a pilot flying low over New Guinea scraped a tree, and crashed. He'd been out here for thirty-two months, longer than any other. If still alive, he won't be for long. Poor guy, he's lost his war. Our own squadron has been out here too long, too. Where pilots used to feel like hell when one of their own didn't make it, there's now, instead, a feeling of resentment. An unnecessary death. Our planes are encountering but minor opposition. As for the troops, I don't know how they're making out. Last night, some bogies dropped by.

April 24 Last night, the task group immediately behind us was attacked. It was for their limited fuel that they didn't reach us. Received a message from the flagship instructing pilots to "concentrate on all fuel stores, as the Japanese are critically short." This was news to those who believed they were short of everything *but*. (J. pilots are now trained to solo in three weeks or less.) Many parked aircraft are observed idle for want of fuel. We're now going around in circles (2 days of it already), awaiting further orders. The drinking water stinks.

April 25 Late tonight we were bothered by one or more subs. Depth charges were dropped by the cans. That was before midnight. Later, in my sack, I could feel the concussion of additional charges. Mercifully, no GQ was sounded. Reliable rumor has it we're now headed for Truk, then Majuro, then Pearl, and finally, praise God, to the States. Would rather skip Pearl. Am sick of that damned hole.

April 26 Mid-afternoon, and just shot down five Bettys.

April 29 It's now 0820, and planes are on their way to Truk. Already this morning we've been attacked by a bunch of Bettys, escorted by

Enemy plane hit while making a dive for the USS *Kitkun Bay* (CVE-71).

[US Navy]

Zeros. Attack ended five minutes ago. The second attack is now coming in. They're five miles off. Should be here any minute now. Now off to the flight deck for the show. Later. Well, we shot one of them down, and maybe two. Yes, two. Now a third has been downed. Always a good show. A torpedo just missed us. Later. Back again, and just now saw another go down, but way off. This could keep up all day. A third attack is now coming in. Another torpedo just passed right *under* us. For some reason, this ship has been singled out for attack. Now back again, and it's 9 AM. No bogies on screen.

April 30 Bogies last night, and they all made it safely home. No wife woke up widowed. This morning, a can sunk a sub. A wallet full of Hawaiian money rose to the surface, and a notebook, too. That was it. Very sad. Sadder still, we lost another pilot today. What? Just learned he was picked up. We've a couple of subs out here who've done wonders picking up lost men. On first day over Truk, and over the ocean, the task force lost seventeen planes. On second day, twenty-three.

May 1 Now on our way back to Majuro. Six battlewagons pounded Ponape all afternoon, each with 125 salvoes from 15 guns. That should have completely wrecked the place. The population, too. So far, battleships haven't had all that much to do in this war. I bet Ponape wasn't bombed from the air in order to give the big ships a kick. It'll help their morale. Obviously, an admiral must think of everything. Rumor, good substantial rumor, has it we'll be hitting the States by May 25. Praise God.

May 6 Pulled out of Majuro today, now with doubts we'll be proceeding to the States. No one will know until we're inspected at Pearl. To date, we've used up 8,000,000 gallons of oil. The Captain says we've traveled a greater distance than any carrier of our class, that is, in the time consumed. Also, seen more action. Everyone is irritable, needs a leave.

May 11 Pulled into Pearl. There's an admiral coming aboard to inspect.

May 14 Believe we're pulling out tomorrow for a five-day cruise—to qualify a new squadron. The new pilots boarded today. No repairs yet. All hope for the States is now out of the question.

May 17 Pulled into Pearl.

May 25 Sandy's here! Guessed from a letter that I was here, too, and he came aboard! Hell of a good time. He's been through a great deal.

May 26 Sandy and six friends boarded for tour of inspection. Stayed for chow.

May 28 Went to Waikiki to meet Sandy and friends. Beer, swim, and talk. Never more open, Sandy, though he couldn't tell me much. He's in an Intelligence department. Says he knows where we're going soon, but couldn't tell me. Five hundred and three ships in convoy.

Fire Drill.

May 29 Pulled out of Pearl. Sandy's on a transport. He's been training for a month on Maui.

June 4 Pulled into Majuro. Fourteen carriers here. Lots of other ships, too. All auxiliary vessels at Kwajalein. Sandy's there. Indications are that we'll be taking the Marianas.

June 5 Two general quarters today. Bogies now within ten miles. Snooping.

June 6 Pulled out of Majuro with task force.

June 7 Man from forward force fell overboard last night. Picked up by one of the cans—thanks to a full moon. First one yet to be rescued. If this war ever ends, I bet he'll never go swimming again.

June 8 Bogies today. Lots of drills, too, like for fire, abandoning ship, and so forth. We strike the Marshall Islands on the 11th, they composed of Guam, Saipan, Tinian, and Rota. Will hit them for three days, then invade Saipan. Guam will be invaded the following day. Then Tinian. For next ten days we'll follow up the troops with continued blasting. Sandy'll be landing on Blue

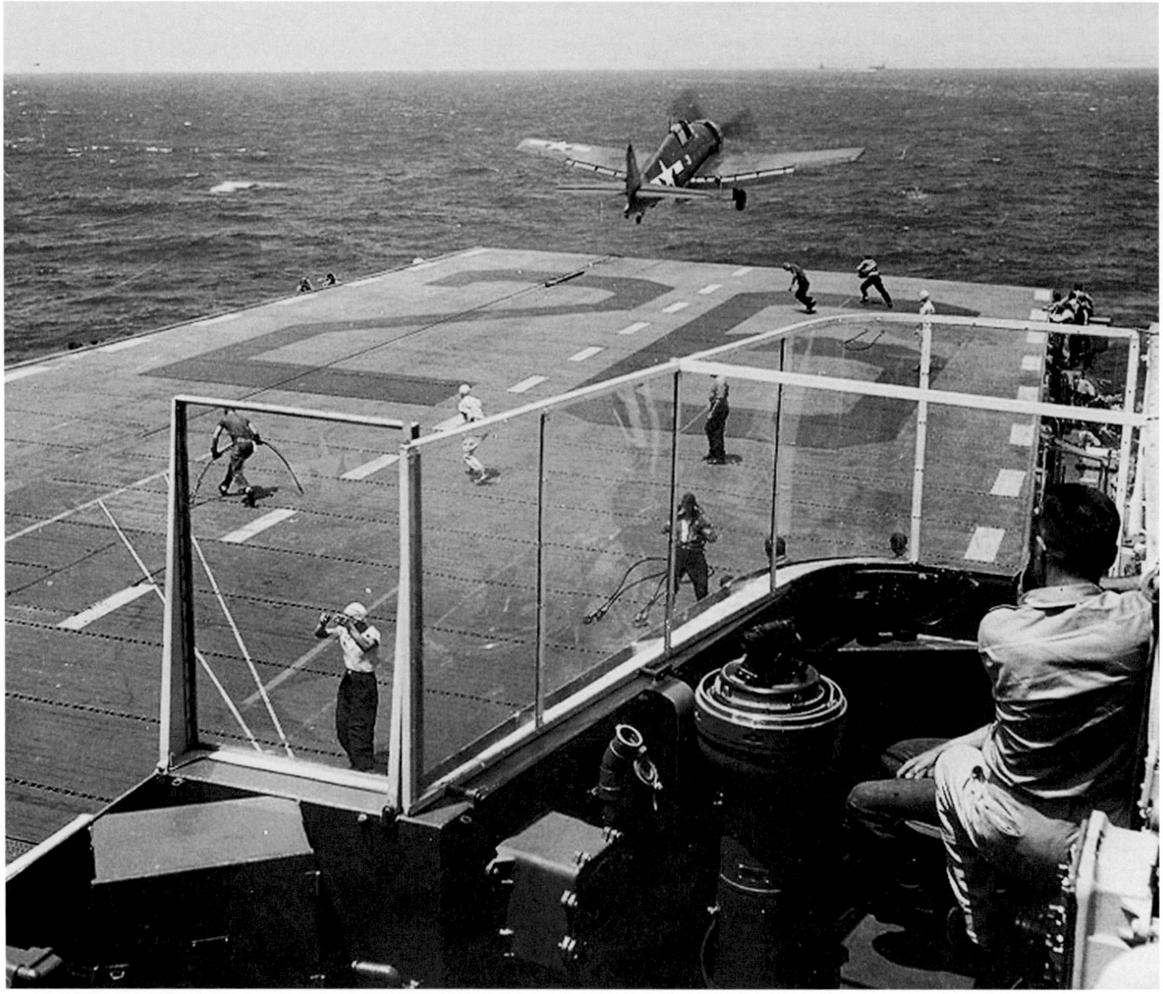

[US Navy]

F6F catapults from flight deck of *Monterey* during operations in the Marianas.

Beach, wherever that is. Saipan, I bet. We're expecting opposition this time, probably from carriers and subs. Yesterday, a second front opened up in Europe.

June 10 We're about 150 miles from Guam. Tomorrow we'll try something new. Rather than launching big dawn attacks, the planes will strike at noon. Nothing all-out, as in the past, but instead, strafing, constant strafing to neutralize their air opposition. We shot down a couple today.

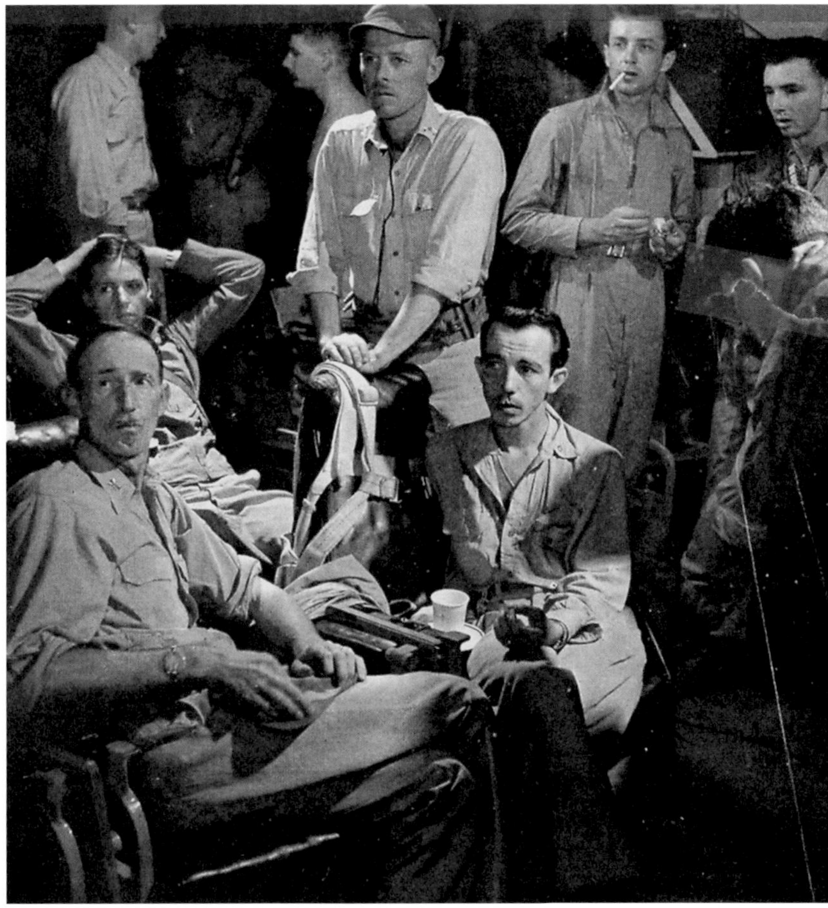

Capt. Ingersoll and Lt. Com. Mehle wait with fighter pilots for news of bombing mission over Tinian.

June 11 We're still about 150 miles from Guam. Either my error or the Admiral's. Would like to know where Sandy is. Early this morning, the water system broke down, and what a hell of a time for that! If hit, there'll be no water for fires. Bogies all about, though less sub opposition than expected.

June 12 Yesterday, a guy threw an old arresting gear overboard. It caught his leg, and he went over the side with the thing. They never picked him up. Bogies all over the place, though no attack until three this morning. We're now forty miles from Tinian. Pilots report that a group of Bettys, rather than fighting, made a hasty landing. Saw men running for shelter before their planes had

After hearing the news from our bomber pilots that they're coming home.

[US Navy]

even stopped moving. One Jap, parachuting over the sea, fell 2,000 feet to his death. Chute never opened. He never surfaced. Yesterday, lots of planes were strafed on the ground, others shot down from the air. This is D-minus 3 day.

June 13 Either the Japs have something up the sleeve, or they're washed up out here. Sandy will soon know. No enemy attack last night. Today, our forces went to within fifteen miles of Saipan, and for first time we could see the battlewagons firing on the island. This is now D-minus 2 day. One of our cans has picked up sixty survivors from a Japanese ship, sunk last night. The can was on her way to bomb Shinto Shimo, and ran into a convoy. Sank most of it. A bulkhead floated by today. Torpedo wakes.

D-Day, Saipan: *(clockwise from right)* USS *Indianapolis* (CA-35), flagship of the Fifth Fleet, and USS *Birmingham* (CL-62) in foreground, bomb Saipan prior to Marine landings. First wave of Marines land (Sandy, among them, was injured when a grenade went off by his foxhole.) Spam sandwiches delivered to battlestations aboard *Monterey*.

[US Navy]

[US Navy]

[Department of Defense (USMC)]

June 14 Yesterday, bombed Saipan all day. Battlewagons. While this was going on, a torpedo, intended for the *Sullivan*, crossed our bow. Too close. Seems we have complete control of these waters. Last night, saw a ship afire. Japanese. Sandy lands tomorrow.

June 15 D-day. Sandy landed this morning, and all day I could hear the battle progressing in his sector. Many casualties, the Captain says. Hope to God he's OK. Subs after us. One sunk. Jap fleet reported headed this way—from Borneo. Have always wanted to meet it, but as Sandy says, that would divert our air power which they rely on. Bogies around, but no business. Tomorrow will mark the ship's first anniversary, and of all things—at this time—what with Sandy and all, I was asked to prepare something for tomorrow's half-hour show. Will do some impersonations and Patrick Henry's speech. Fiddle while Rome burns.

June 16 GQ last night. Shot down eight planes. The crossfire on one of them in flames was especially beautiful. Earlier, one of our commanders was shot down by his own men. His IFF was off. Also, our squadron leader had to parachute. Engine trouble. Picked up by a can. Jap fleet reported headed this way. Sandy won't like that. It's going sixteen knots. If they're serious, we should see them tomorrow. Have to put on that skit this PM. I wonder how S. is making out?

June 18 Yesterday, cancelled all raids on Guam because of possible presence of Jap fleet. GQ last night, but bogies within five miles only. Steamed westward all night to get in touch with Jap fleet, but without success. Guess they must have turned back. This morning, our planes shot down a Betty some forty miles from ship. A sub may have been sunk a couple of nights ago. Fifty depth charges.

June 19 For three or four days now, we and their fleet have been baiting one another, they not moving into our range, and we not daring to go so deep as to be hit by their bombers from the Philippines. This see-saw play is tough on the morale, knowing as we do what a battle could mean. We'd rather be home. Indications are we'll meet the fleet either today or tomorrow. All ships unprepared for battle have been ordered to retire. All battlewagons and cruisers have been positioned in battle formation. The Captain, last night, was in here looking at the weather maps, and said we'd better put on our "lucky shoes" in the morning. I'd like either to fight or retire. This see-saw stuff is no good. Yesterday, a body floated by. Few minutes ago, we shot down a Tony.[1]

It's now two in the morning, and we've just survived a third torpedo attack. Well, hell, these are their waters. Their fleet's about 300 miles away, hiding in a weather front. (I'd hate to be

1. Japanese fighter plane. Unlike the Zero, the Tony had protective armor for pilot and gas tank.

MJ on stage, reciting Patrick Henry's speech in one minute, twelve seconds, falling down at concluding line, "Give me liberty or give me death," at which point, he's pulled off the stage by his legs.

Officers attending the show.

[US Navy]

A bomb just misses the USS *Bunker Hill* (CV-17). Japanese plane at left is missing its tail and about to crash. Photo taken from *Monterey*, June 19, 1944.

their admiral's aerologist, should it suddenly lift.) All of them safely returning, our pilots—from all carriers—shot down twenty planes, two of them credited to the *Monterey*. At one time, there were a couple of Japs parachuting into the sea. That's always a sight. The *Hornet* and the *Bunker Hill* escaped with near misses. Thirty yards or so. Those tasting the *Monterey* were shot down just in time, their torpedoes going down with them. A heartbreaking waste, those pilots must have thought. Their subs are all over the place. I'd now like to go after their fleet, and be done with it. This hide-and-seek gets us nowhere. Right now, another big attack is coming in from the west. I hope to hell all's OK with Sandy.

It's now 8 AM, and we've just recovered from the fifth attack of the day. Three torpedo attacks, and two from the air. Bombs. Interesting, those bomb attacks. The *Bunker Hill* and *Wasp* are welding their seams, loosened by near misses. Two men fell—or were blown—overboard. A hundred and eighty-three enemy planes were splashed today, and twenty-three probables. Quite a day! Hitting the sack now. Expect to be roused. It's now 10 PM.

June 20 A quiet night. Firing on the horizon, though, continued until dawn, which means some other task force was getting their eye. Yesterday, our gunners accounted for three planes, one of them nearly splashing on the deck. Don't know how many our pilots got. At the moment (0700) we're heading west. We're 141 deg. longitude, the farthest west we've ever been. Means we're definitely going after their fleet. Today might be more than interesting.

Twenty minutes ago (3 PM) the Japanese fleet was at long last sighted: 14 deg. north, 135 deg. east, and some 240 miles away. Our snooper planes observed two enemy groups, twelve ships in one, ten in the other. So few. Obviously, more are somewhere in the fog. At the moment, their carriers and cruisers are refueling. Ideal time to attack, I'd say. Our planes have just now taken off, not to return until dark. Means it'll be first time we'll have had night landings. They'll not have an easy time of it. This is the big one. Of course, God's part Japanese. One's apt to forget that. We have twenty-two subs not many miles away (350 or so) and they'll be doing *their* jobs, too. We'll probably have the big naval engagement tomorrow. High time. One mustn't forget that that's what we've all been looking for, and waiting for, now for so long. Our position is now 200 miles east of theirs. They're hiding, still in a warm stationary front. Excellent hideout weather. Rain, low ceiling, and so forth. Tough offensive conditions though.

June 21 Well our planes took off, at least. It wasn't the big show we'd all been looking for. A bit of their fleet was discovered, that's all. For some odd reason it was out in the open. We did inflict a direct hit on a big carrier, though, and on a tanker, too. All results not yet known. Intense fire from their battlewagons. Our task force lost many planes, mostly for their having run out of gas. Lost about sixty, and that's a lot. They had to land late at night. Those out of gas had to plunge into the sea, some right before our eyes. One plane that made it was so empty that it couldn't even taxi up the flight deck. A Jap Val[1] was in our formation and tried to land on a carrier! Gave the wrong signal, thereby revealing its identity.

1. The Val was the first Japanese aircraft to drop bombs on Pearl Harbor.

Fires on *Bunker Hill* from planes crashing on the deck. One of our planes is missing. All day today pilots are being picked up here and there. This morning, a second attack was launched. No results in yet. We're still heading west, but whether or not we'll move in with the battleships—to mow 'em down—that I don't know. The next few hours will tell. They're retreating, damnit. We could lose them. This afternoon, a guy from a can who tried to commit suicide was transferred to this ship. Now he *will* succeed! GQ at one AM this morning. We're all quite sleepy, and I've the damned midwatch tonight. We shot down a Betty this afternoon. Near misses killed lots of guys on *Bunter Hill* and the *Hornet*, or was it the *Wasp*? One guy lost his head at the shoulders. Well, where else?

June 24 Well, the Japanese fleet beat it, and that puts an end to that, if not to them. An expensive disappointment. On the brighter side, at least half the pilots were picked up, including ours. He was hauled aboard yesterday. Of eighteen planes shot down by our force, we're credited with five. That's pretty good. The guy who went nuts, the one from the can who tried to take his life, he isn't eating. But then, he'd be nuts *to*! Worms. Our patrol has shot down thirty planes. Today we strike Pagan Island, northernmost of the Marianas, then on to Eniwetok to load on provisions. Fresh flour, I hope. Just as the ship's Anniversary Show was going on (I was to do some impersonations), bogies began closing in, and the audience scattered in a hundred directions. Am making signs for Officer Country[1] with funny drawings. Good practice.

June 29 Was lucky enough to be one of four drawn from V-3 Division (drawn by lot) to make it to Eniwetok for a beer party. Three warm beers, a downpour, and a swim to a sunken picket boat. Picked up a beautiful Jap shell, but on way back to shore, a big fish came after me. Konked the thing with it (was more frightened than by any Jap) and lost it. I was very unhappy.

1. Restricted sleeping quarters for Officers.

Lt. Gerald R. Ford stands next to a fellow officer *(below, on left.)* Ford served aboard *Monterey* as Gunnery Officer and Asst. Navigator. He was also our Athletic Director and organized basketball games in the forward elevator *(right)*.

[Gerald R. Ford Library]

[Gerald R. Ford Library]

Baseball.

Flightdeck football.

USS *Monterey*, V-3 Division, July 1944 (MJ in front row, far right).

June 30 Have pulled out of Eniwetok for some unknown place. Doubt that we'll be returning to Saipan. Reliable rumor has it we'll be returning to the States by December.

July 2 On the fourth of July we strike Chichi Shima, and Lo Shima, 500 miles from Japan. Somehow, knowing Sandy's on Saipan, poor guy, and after that Jap attack on our fleet, and after so many months of this shit, my enthusiasm's all but gone sour. The Shimas should be a real scrap. Eight thousand casualties on Saipan. Jesus, how's Sandy, I wonder?

July 5 Attacked Chichi Shima. Good results. Sank 3 cruisers, and downed 30/40 planes. Our own cruisers bombed the island.

Same ol' stuff. I wanna go home for a rest. Everyone else does, too, even the damned Captain. The crew needs a radical change. Crew unhealthy. Skin diseases, short tempers, sex starved, and bored, bored even by the enemy. Planes attacked Pagon Island on way to Saipan area. Our ships not attacked. Three quarters of Saipan is now ours, but at an awful price. I feel sick. What about Sandy? Yesterday, a couple of planes strafed a bunch of Jap soldiers in a narrow valley. Pilots counted over a thousand dead. Am smoking too much, and must slow down. Find it relaxing. Dentist tomorrow. Should be home by December. Can't believe it, but after a leave, I'd like to return to this ship. Lots of damage was done at Pagon Island (ships sunk, etc.), but a TBF, which had to land in the water, exploded, killing three of our men. Pilot and crew. Later, a *Monterey* fighter was shot down, splashing the pilot not ten miles off Pagon. Miraculously, picked up. Last evening, we were within 8 miles of Pagon, and what a sight she was: a black shadow heaving up from the waters. Where in hell were their coastal guns?

July 6 My birthday pretty soon. More attacks.

July 7 Attacks on Rota. Sunk a sub. Bogies and GQ at 0100 of the 6th. Tough getting up. Fed up. No planes lost at Rota. GQ sounded at breakfast. Had just sat down. Shot down six Japs. Traua (my Aerological Officer) just got orders to report to the States for a 30-day leave, then on to Brisbaine, Australia. He's a very happy man. Three hours later, it was cancelled. Very unhappy. He's now navigator, too.

July 9 Today I'm 21 years old.

July 20 For past two weeks, we've been hitting Guam and Rota. Few air attacks on us, as the Japs have no fields left, bombed that they've been on Rota, Tinian, and Guam. Saipan's been taken, though not without great loss. Am impatient to get to Eniwetok for a letter from Sandy. He'll write. D-Day tomorrow—for Guam. As Saipan taught us a lesson, we're now bombing the hell out of G. At night, the destroyers blast it. Off and on, we approach within 7 miles of her. On one occasion, her shore batteries opened fire. Much talk of the States by August, even from the Captain, who's doing his best to get us there. He'd be the first off, I bet. Everyone's ill-humored, needs a big rest. What I want most is privacy. A pup tent on the Sahara would do just fine. Little typhoons here and there. This is the season. Definitely, we're going to Pearl for repairs. Boilers on the blink, again. Should Sandy receive a commission, he'll be home in few weeks. God, how I hope he's OK.

July 22 Pulled into Saipan this afternoon. Tinian, 30 miles distant, was being divebombed and shelled as we passed by. Quite a sight, but damned moving, too, as Sandy was there. I can see why it was so tough an island to capture. Tonight, tried to send him a message, but was persuaded to wait until morning. Well, hell, I

Sandy on Tinian.

was *ordered* to wait. Communications Officer has the heart of a slingshot. There's mail coming aboard. Pulling out tomorrow. We're unloading all bombs, replacing them with "flyable duds." Definitely, no doubt about it, we're going to Pearl, and then on to the States, here's praying. Am too worried about Sandy to enjoy the beauty of this island. The entire task force is here, exposing us to great danger. The commanding Admiral may be the only man here who isn't nervous.

July 26 Taking hell of a long time getting back to Eniwetok and Pearl. The squadron may be relieved at Eniwetok. If so, the States becomes a certainty. Sandy's busted eardrums will keep him from a Tinian invasion.[1] A V-mail from him, delivered at Saipan. Never got that message off to him. God knows I tried. Mum worried. Surely, he's written home. Am relieved beyond thought. All I can do is smile. Danny's somewhere in India. A few sub scares the other day. Gunnery practice this AM. I miss the real thing. No potatoes for 4 weeks. Horrible food. Powdered eggs taste like urinated flour. Worms in the bread.

August Pearl.

September 2 We're now well out to sea again, following three long weeks, and more, at Pearl. Repairs. Needless to say, we didn't repair to the States. My Officer Traua has departed, replaced by a Lt. Choun. Before leaving, Traua gave me an exam for First Class, and I got a 3.7 on the thing, which equals 92%. That was very much like Traua, as my limited time in Second Class didn't warrant my going up so soon. Also, he let me use a book. We may be winning the war, but not because we're saints. The bureau in Washington must pass on it, too. I'm in no hurry. However low my esteem for Pearl, must confess I had a good rest. Needed it, too. Had 48 hours at Camp Andrews, a rest-and-recreation camp. Tents. Eight to a tent. Nothing but food, sleep, and little games. Nearly everyone soon had enough of it, though. Good to be out to sea again.

1. It didn't.

September 3 Was almost rammed by a cruiser this morning. Missed our stern by fewer than ten feet. The crew was told to stand by for a ram. Quite a sight, everyone dashing up to the flight deck—toward the bow—some of them screaming. I almost shat. Bombed Wake Island today. First time. It's been neutralized, though, for months, and the inhabitants are starving. They've little fighting spirit. It was more of a practice affair, our using rockets for first time, though the pilots, also, did drop some conventional bombs. The few ships in our force—2 cans, 3 cruisers, and the *Monterey*—received no air opposition. About all the Japs could throw at us were chicken bones. Got 3 letters from Fran White, who's getting married. Back at Pearl, the Captain was awarded the Legion of Merit. Nothing for me. Four flyers were credited with sinking a big carrier in battle of the Philippines, awarded Navy Crosses. Hot as hell on flight deck, attending the ceremony. Not good for the morale. Looks like I'll be putting in my full 18 months before getting home. Palau will be next, then the Philippines. Admiral Halsey's on the *New Jersey*. Big stuff. Europe looks great.

September 20 I don't seem to write so often any more. Lots may be lost, but the urge is no longer here. I now write only on important occasions. The present occasion finds us on the eve of striking Manila Bay (northern Philippines), a strike that's a good 2 months ahead of schedule. Encouraging. For first time, land bombers will be in position to get at us. If boredom's our main enemy, then that's pretty good news. Considering Luzon has 73 air strips (the Japs, of course, could choose to retreat, thereby saving planes for attacks on Japan proper), tomorrow may hold lots of welcomed interest. Can't deny I'm nervous. While at Pearl for repairs, the invasion of Palau took place. We also missed the strike on the southern Philippines. Those were the first engagements we've missed since way back I've forgotten when, and right now I don't give a damn one way or the other. The south Philippine Sea offered no opposition. What's more, we're no longer Task Force 58, but 38. We're 38.1. There are 4 groups that make up the whole

[Gerald R. Ford Library]

Award ceremony on flight deck.

of 38. Halsey's in command, and he's a daredevil. (Some guy, exhausted and "asiatic," threatened an officer the other day, bawled like a baby, etc., and was given an M.D. We've lost several that way, one of them a straight jacket case.) I look forward to tomorrow. We're now near the Philippines, though not yet sighted. Our aim is to sink ships in the harbor. Twenty-three U.S. subs are now milling around its entrance, to torpedo them should they decide to pull out. Following day we'll hit the airstrips. Lost a pilot today when his plane made a forced landing in the drink. Sandy also fought on Tinian. Saipan and Tinian, both, poor guy. He seems depressed. I've sent $455 home. Took—and passed—exam for First Class P.O.[1] It's now being approved, or disapproved, in Washington. Traua gave me a 3.8 "proficiency in rating" for half year ending in June, and a 317 for "leader of men." Little

1. Petty Officer.

will Washington know I mostly bluff. Forecasting is nine-tenths intuition, and one-tenth science. This ship left Philly a year ago tomorrow, west longitude time. Big disappointment not going home, though I may now be sure of a thirty days' leave when the time is ripe. Had the Japs been bombed as many times as we've talked of going home, the war would long since have been over. We're sailing with the *Hornet*, the *Wasp*, and the *Cowpens*, plus twelve cans and three cruisers. I hope we meet their fleet again.

September 21 It's now 9:30 AM, and Radio Manila has gone off the air. It's now 9:40, and an 8-ship convoy has been sighted off Corregidor Bay. Now 10:10, and the ackack is heavy from Manila. Many ships in harbor. Dropped lots of torpedoes. All day we've been under a low ceiling. Also, a gentle rain at times. Right now, it's a pleasure to escape troubles from the Japs. Later. Not so many ships sunk in harbor as had been hoped. This war could go on and on, I'm afraid. All we know for sure is that we'll win it. It wasn't always that way.

September 22 Launched planes at dawn, the J.'s attacking us right off the bat. At 11:00 AM, as this is being written, it's alot more severe than when their fleet met us some time ago. They aimed five bombs at us: two near misses, and three wide of the mark. One plane strafed us, hitting eighteen men. Oddly, none killed. Even odder, no suicide pilots among them. Am not registering a formal complaint. Perfect ceiling for divebombing. Only one shot down, though, and one earlier, too. Their near misses are always quite a jolt. Our planes are just now returning. Heroic flyers. Ours and their, both.

September 23 No attacks last night. Today, though, a four-engine bomber was shot down around noon, at 20,000 feet. It failed to dive. Seems too bad we robbed him of that bold and final fling. I nearly always find action a satisfying adventure, while in the States, I'd cringe at the dive of so little as a wren. We didn't aim well

Jap torpedo bomber hit by a 5-inch shell.

yesterday, and are now on our way to Saipan for provisions. Rough weather during attacks. Looks like we'll be spending lots of time with the Philippines.

September 24 Yesterday, we were in sight of the Philippines, and if I do say so myself, they were quite a sight. After so long a hungering for an end to it all, the sight tasted like Victory. Swallowed whole. Well, anyway, no troubles last night. Enemy plane shot down today. It's now somewhat later, and here we are again in sight of land. Soon she'll be ours, and then on to Japan. A can delivered seventeen bags of mail; two letters from home. Danny wounded in India. We lost a pilot today. After a safe landing on the Philippines, he took off for the hills. After landing, he remained in radio contact with his squadron commander, who then shot up the grounded plane, thereby keeping it from Jap hands. We're now heading for Manus, the Admiralties. Will arrive by 29th. I want to be home more and more. Am fed up with it all, and most of all, I'm fed up with the war.

October 2 We've been in the Admiralties now for four days, at Manus, and this is where Traua is stationed. Came aboard, but I missed him. In time, he'll go to the Philippines. Had liberty on an islet (four beers), and it was quite a day. A jungle of uprooted mess. Mud and debris all over the place. Drank in a ditch. Drunks and fights. Chaos. Better than a circus. Pulled out today—for Formosa, I guess. Okinawa, maybe. If opposition isn't extensive, we may strike Japan proper, and Formosa, too. Aboard are fifty-seven *extra* tons of bombs. A hit would blow us sky high. Without doubt, this'll be the biggest job yet. Everyone's a bit expectant. Halsey's a fighter. If worse comes to worst, he'll be a dead hero. The rest of us just dead. So far, we've lost six men to madness. Three days ago, a guy went nuts, cut his wrists, and then bawled like a baby when someone pointed to a finger he'd sworn had been removed. Yesterday, a guy threatened an officer, threatened to get him topside some time. Got five days bread-and-water. The crew is bone tired, edgy, too, particularly those of us aboard since last September. Put on a skit last night (hanger deck), imitating the Exec. Officer and the Captain. It went off semi-well. Not as well as other times. We all need a leave. On Broadway, I'd have been thrown out of the house.

October 8 For past three or four days we've been under the influence of a 981 low, its center about 300 miles off, and the seas are tremendous. Though all flights have been cancelled, Halsey's heading right into it. The ship has rolled as much as 26 degrees. At supper last night, she took about 8 heavy rolls, and I never laughed so hard in months. Four hundred broken cups. Food all over the place. Expressions of fear, anger, boredom, amusement, and disgust. God, it was wonderful, everyone and everything all over the place, but now we'll be eating off the deck for awhile, and it's not so funny. We're fueling now, and tonight we begin the run for the Nance Islands, 200 miles south of Japan. We'll strike in a couple of days. That's what Halsey says. But there's that low pressure up there! I'd sit this one out. Then on to Formosa, Luzon, and the rest of the Philippines. The Phils will be invaded on the 19th or 21st. Task Group 38.1 will cover

Moving 'up the ladder' toward Tokyo.

[Pictorial History of the Second World War, Wm. H. Wise Co. Inc., v4, p. 1768]

the invasion (Adm. McCain is our boss), while the other task groups continue hitting Luzon. Should the Jap fleet be sighted, the *Monterey* and another CVL will go in with the battlewagons and cruisers, etc.—more or less expendable. The *Cowpens* may be the other one. That I'd find quite interesting had I not lost my interest. The last two engagements with the fleet have made me really quite nervous. The nearer Japan we get, the tougher they become, and Halsey becomes more daring. He's a good man, but a daredevil. The place on Luzon is Appari. We invade at Leyte!

Heading for Leyte.

October 11 Yesterday, Okinawa was hit, that island off southern Japan, and we did a great job. Sank one big cruiser, a smaller one, a can, and damaged some other ships. In the PM there was nothing left to sink. We had snoopers around for most of the day, and three Bettys were shot down. Though these snoopers weren't in sight of the fleet, we were on GQ all day from three in the morning until eight that night. Had a GQ at 2:30 this morning, but sadly, the Japs turned back. If damage to our rest could win this war, they'd be in Washington by now. It's always irritating to be unnecessarily roused, and particularly so for a snooper. Returned to the sack for an hour's sleep—before reveille. Today we hit Luzon. No opposition yet, but they have our position, that's for sure. It's unbelievable—our not having more action so near their homeland. Were they off San Francisco, even Edith Mason would be throwing eggs.[1] Tomorrow we'll hit Formosa. They won't care for that at all. We expect troubles. About six hundred planes left for the China coast last night, and then returned. Also, we sank six subs. Philippines to be invaded on the 20th.

1. Edith Mason was a little old maid from my hometown.

We'll supply air support till the 28th. Could be the longest week of my life. Though distracted, everyone's irritable and homesick. A message just now arrived asking how well we're equipped for "northern weather?" That must mean the Kuriles, and that means I'll be kicked out of the balloonroom. Actually, I'd not mind being cold for awhile. Our new officer, Choun, is good off-watch, but old-maidish on duty. He's all for the enlisted man, though, and has a fair sense of humor. Knows his stuff, and that's fine, because I don't know mine. The rasonde machine remains incomprehensible. Willkie died the other day, and that's really tough.

October 12 Yesterday, I mean today, we invaded—no, let's begin again. (Am writing this on the 13th—amid a fracas.) Today, as of the 12th, we hit Formosa. Nothing happened to us during the day. Good results. At dusk, though, planes came in, a swarm, really (about an hour ago), and Jesus, there's more going on, all kinds of action, than I've ever seen. Just shot down 2 planes. One that was burning, flew a half-mile for a dive on the *Hornet* (or *Wasp*), and plunged into the sea just a few feet short. The cruiser *Canberra* was hit, and is now being towed by the *Wichita*. Four cruisers from another big force are now on their way to take their places. A Jap on a raft signaled one of our ships to pick him up. Don't know if we bothered. Hope so. Their planes were *everywhere*. Wherever I looked, there was another one. Never a show quite like it. Also, there's a wind picking up. Fifty knots across the deck. On the flight deck, I find myself saying, "Jesus, how fine!" As a pacifist, that's hard to hear. It must be that nearly anything's better than monotony. It isn't fine at all, not really. The Captain just squarkyboxed that the *Monterey* is credited with 6 shot down. I believe it. They were falling all over the place. He said that the *Wasp* and the *Hornet* ducked some torpedoes, and that we missed one, too, just forward of the bow. News to me. There's a bogie dead ahead right now, 6 miles off. Will continue later.

October 14 No more excitement last night. The *Canberra* got a nasty hit—forward engineroom. Glad the Jap lived to see it. Was downed a minute later. In fact, only one enemy plane *didn't* go down. Those 4 cruisers we thought were to join us, well, they haven't shown up. Right now, we're miserably protected; 1 cruiser, 8 cans, and the 4 carriers. Our planes today aren't hitting Formosa, but instead patrolling the waters around the *Canberra*. She's being towed. A fast-going tugboat is on its way to take over. Last night, our own ackack flak wounded 30 men on a destroyer. This morning, a message was sent over from the flagship that their Jap interpreter reports there's an enemy attack planned for us today. I think he's been misled; for unless hundreds of planes are sent in, it'd be suicide. (Of course, they could all be kamikazi planes!) On night of 12th, we used smoke screens for first time. Spooky.

October 15 Yesterday, at dusk, the Japs came in, again. Saw six of them downed. There were others, too, that made for beautiful fires. Some, of course, go down without exploding. The gunners always feel cheated. The cruiser *Houston* was twice hit, and is listing. Abandoning ship wasn't all that easy, what with high seas and the dark of night. For awhile we were going to finish her off with our own torpedoes, but then all flooding was plugged above the third deck, and there's talk of saving her. Mournful sight. She's being towed at 5 knots, and the *Canberra* at 4. She must have lost many men. Looks like we'll be going through the same thing tonight. Milling around like this is an invitation to disaster. They kept us up last night until ten, when I finally hit the sack. Today, too, they've been around. Our flyers shot down nine, the four carriers a total of 51. Grandfather Paine told Mum the Japanese women were the most beautiful in the world. There'll be lots of tortured beauties come sundown, when the word is passed. The *Wasp* lost two pilots. At five, a bunch of dive bombers dropped in, and the *Wasp* enjoyed a near miss. Got two of them. The *Cowpens* has been detached to escort the *Canberra* and *Houston* back to the States, lucky shits. Initially, the *Monterey* was assigned that duty, but because we've no more rockets aboard, lost out. I guess many lives were lost last night, or was it the night before? Am all mixed up today. There's nothing more sad, no lonelier a sight, than that of empty rafts floating by, unless it could be the sight of a lifebelt fully inflated, and no one there. That's how it's been all day. Some lucky few were picked up. We're now on our way to fuel, which we should have been doing yesterday. Maybe that's why I'm all mixed up. Whatever day it is, the last two have been pure hell. Doubt that they'll be returning tonight. Though I do enjoy the spectacle, and have to remain up until midnight, anyway, I now sort of hope they stay put, everyone being so pooped and all. Jumpy, too. Short fuses. The past few days have been hell.

October 16 We were supposed to invade the Philippines, beginning tomorrow, but our subs are reporting that the Jap fleet is steaming toward Formosa. Should that be accurate, we'll head for *there* instead, as their ships are our main concern. This, too, could be interesting. The invasion, though, will still come off on the 20th. The enemy is claiming fourteen carriers sunk, along with one battleship, a cruiser, and so forth. If true, then the *Monterey*'s at the bottom of the sea, and Edith Mason, too. If their fleet's coming out for a scrap, I have to think they do believe their claims. Sort of sad. No troubles last night. That Jap report has now been confirmed, and the Captain just told us we're now on our way to meet them. We'll try to lure them into a trap, that is, if we have one. He didn't say. In any event, we've 25 subs ready to strike, should they pull a retreat. By morning, we should be 200 miles short of the confrontation. Nimitz is reporting that Task Force 38 has been "badly mauled." That could give the Japs the confidence they need. The *Houston*, under attack all day, has just now received yet another torpedo, but is still in tow. Half her 1400 crew has been picked up. We're now steaming at 25 knots. I really do look forward to this.

October 18 Apparently, the Japs have discovered our fleet's not all that impaired. Wouldn't you know it! Am really disappointed. We're now back to Luzon, of all dull holes. Guess we'll be going to Leyte tomorrow—to soften her up for invasion. Yesterday, one of our pilots bailed out near the ship, and his plane took a beautiful nosedive. Picked up by a can, and back on board within the hour. We're expecting the J.'s to attack us today, but who knows? Hope so. Guess I'll be home in March, as by then it'd be 18 months at sea.

October 24 For a few days now, we've been on our way to Ulithe, off Yap. Were supposed to bomb her today, but suddenly there's word that Task Group 38.3, in the Philippines, is under heavy attack, that the carrier *Princeton*'s been bombed (burning up, and out of control), and that 4 Jap battlewagons, several cruisers, 7 or more carriers, etc., are steaming here and there *among* the Phils. We've just now reversed course. Should take about two days to get there, by which time it may be too late. The *Princeton*'s bum luck may delay our returning to the States. More and more in this war, if it's not one thing, it's another. Could be months, even, before we head home. Am writing the ship's history, from November to March, for the Bureau.

October 25 Yesterday, the *Princeton* was hit by a good-sized bomb. Late in the day, the crew abandoned her, then scuttled her. Mid-day, a cruiser came alongside to pick up equipment and men, I guess, but instead, 400 of her *own* men got blown around when the *Princeton* exploded. The *P.* is a *Monterey* class carrier. Right now, the Japs are on the other side of the Phils, and their whole fleet, what remains of it, is milling around. At least 12 battlewagons are there, and today we're going all out to locate their exact position. I don't know what the *Princeton*'s sinking holds for us all, as far as the States is concerned. Now we may never get home. The chow stinks, small portions, too (that should be a mercy, I suppose), and there's limited water. On the 22nd, I was in the Navy two years. The Captain just now on the squarky said, "The fate of

USS *Princeton* (CVL-23) explodes after being hit by a bomb. The USS *Birmingham* (CL-62) is by her side.

the Japanese navy, and incidentally our own, may well be sealed within the next few hours." Seems that everything they've got is somewhere ready for a fight. Last night, salvoes were exchanged, though not between them and *our* force. We're steaming at 28 knots. They're hiding among the islands. We've 15 tankers out here, usually no more than 4 or 5. We'll be there later in the day. It's now 9 AM. At 1330, we reversed course, and are now heading for Leyte. I don't get it. Their battlewagons beat it. That's their game: emerge, shoot around a bit, and then retreat. Tough on us all, what with such awful food, and all. The CVE is under salvo attack right now, near Leyte, by yet another Jap force (didn't know they had another), and that's where we're headed.

USS *St. Lô* (CVE-63) explodes after being hit by *kamikaze* plane, losing 114 of her crew.

[US Navy]

October 29 Today, we're pulling into Ulithe, near Yap, for 2 or 3 days. Besides the *Princeton* being sunk, so were two other carriers, the *Gambier Bay* and *St. Lô*. One of them was caught right in the middle (more or less) of the Jap task force, and there's not a single survivor. The other, she exploded after an enemy plane crash-landed the entire length of the ship, toppling over on to the foc'sle.[1] Also, 2 cans were sunk, and one destroyer escort. Several other escort carriers were damaged, but America's losses were small in comparison to theirs. Anyway, so we say.

November 2 We were supposed to hang around here until the 6th, but last night sudden orders arrived and we're now pulling out. It's bright and early in the morning. The Jap fleet's on the move. Anyway, that's what I think. While we've been here, the carriers *Belleau Wood*, *Franklin*, and *Intrepid*, have been hit. With the *Monterey*'s good luck, we'll never make it back to the States. The cruiser *Denver* was also hit. Things are really picking up around here. The *Franklin* and *Belleau Wood* were hit by suicide planes, which the J's are now calling their "Secret Weapon". Wish they'd keep it a secret. The kamikazi pilots have pledged their lives to the destruction of all enemy carriers. No trees to hide behind, either. Quite honestly, I'm willing to go home at any time.

1. Foc'sle (forecastle) is the upper deck area of the bow.

[US Navy]

USS *Franklin* (CV-13) listing from *kamikaze* strike that killed 724 and wounded 265 of her crew.

November 4 Are now on our way to the Philippines. Looks like MacArthur has insufficient air power, and that this hurried exit from Ulithi is to knock out his troublesome Japs. Four of our destroyers were sunk last week, and last night, a sub put a torpedo into the cruiser *Reno*. She was on our starboard side. I was asleep at the time and didn't hear of it till now. Should this sort of thing continue, we'll soon not be the mighty fleet we were. Sandy's in Hawaii. Danny's under Mountbatten. The Captain spoke tonight, urging everyone to be more on the alert than ever before. Said that the Japs have brought in some 1,000/1,500 more planes, and that kamikazis will certainly be among them. Said that the next two days may be rough ones, and "I'm choosy about whom I have aboard this ship, and I don't want any slanteyed bastards. That's all." My grandfather Paine thought their eyes the most beautiful in the world. Rather than the usual "That's all," Captain Hundt would have concluded, "And may God bless you all." We'll be striking northern Luzon in the morning. MacArthur now has most of Leyte in his pocket, and Samar, too, but there's considerable air opposition. He keeps whining for help. The cruiser *Reno*, commissioned but 5 months

A photo I picked up in the water while ashore at Leyte, June 1945.

ago, is running on one screw. That's not good. Also, her steering wheel is on the bum, and she's going in circles. Dad's painting Marquand sometime this month. More tomorrow, maybe.

November 6 Last night it was GQ the whole night long. It's now 0500, and everyone is pooped. Cartons of dead sandwiches distributed for breakfast. What's more, bogies never came nearer than 56 miles, just close enough to keep track of us. They'll attack today, I imagine. Yesterday, our squadron shot down 14, and destroyed 4 on the ground. We lost a swell pilot. Also, a suicide plane crashed into the *Lexington*, hitting her bridge. A second one splashed, just missing the new carrier, *Ticonderoga*. A third one was shot down in its suicide plunge. Interesting folks, these Japanese. I wonder what may happen today? If the ship's crippled, I'll have to destroy this diary. It's illegal to keep one, and I can see why. Luckily, my GQ station is elastic. I have the run of the flight deck. Will be up there running, either this way or that, depending on the position of the plunger. Their Secret Weapon is extremely effective. One must hand it to them.

November 7 Tomorrow I hope F.D.R. is reelected. Yesterday, bogies right overhead, and never attacked us. Odd. I don't understand them sometimes. Reliable sources have it that after refueling today, it's off to Formosa (more strikes) and then on to Tokyo. We hit Tokyo on the 16th and 17th. The Captain's been heard to say that the squadron's to be relieved in January. The elevator's in terrible shape. Our water system is even worse. The ship has been out here now for 15 months. He believes that after Tokyo, we'll head for the States. Oh mother of Jacob, wouldn't that be fine! We all need a breather.

November 10 Now again the Jap fleet's been sighted in the Philippines. Four battlewagons, 6 cruisers, 3 carriers, and some cans. All night we've been going after it at 26 knots. First thing that comes to mind is our boilers. Hope they can stand this speed. Yesterday, even the flight deck elevator got stuck. These problems may delay the Tokyo job. Someone fell overboard two days ago, while refueling, and drowned in rough seas. It was tough to see him splashing around for 2 or 3 minutes, surrounded by lifejackets and rafts. He has a wife.

November 11 Today, discovered, and quite by accident, that my exam for First Class, taken August 1st, is still in the Exec's office. Mislaid. With that sort of efficiency, we'll never win this war. Had I not cheated on the thing, would be really pissed off. Inexcusable. What the hell, though. All I need, really, is the cash, and I don't need that. As usual, the Jap fleet was neither here nor there. Some damage, though, was done to their shipping. Luzon tomorrow. It was before MacArthur's S.O.S. that I saw the message re raids on Tokyo and Yokahama, planned for the 17th. Obviously, there'll now be a delay of a week or more. The ship's in terrible shape, spirits are low, and I smoke too much.

November 19 We've been down around Leyte for a week. Tokyo delayed. Boring. No bogies, not a one. Some enemy ships have been sunk, though, thereby sweetening MacArthur's life. He'll have an easier time of it now, not that that should make for sweeter dreams aboard this ship. No one likes him. Today we bomb Luzon, softening her up for the invasion of the 25th. Scuttlebutt has it we'll be returning to the States in January. The *Bunker Hill,* out here precisely two weeks longer than we, has already returned. Considering the fact she's returning without a torpedo in her side, that's encouraging. Never have I wanted so dearly to be home.

November 20 Mum's birthday. Attacked last night. Bagged one. The aft guns got her. Wasn't a suicide dive, thank God. Am no longer getting such a kick out of this. Funny thing, we're now on our way—AGAIN—to Ulithi, this time for elevator repairs. So to hell with Tokyo, and Luzon too. Wake me up when they fall.

Bored.

November 27 Pulled into Ulithi a few days ago. Was on Shore Patrol, or more precisely, Jungle Patrol. The Captain's told us we'd be home by January. Almost a certainty. The carriers *Intrepid* and *Cabot* have just now been hit by suicide planes. That could foul up the States. Captain said the *Monterey* has put in more miles in Jap waters than any carrier save the *Enterprise*. I believe it. Adm. Halsey wants us for one more job. I believe *that*, too. Will there be no end to this? We'll be pulling out on the first for invasion of Luzon, but damn these suicide planes. Most of the carriers have now been hit. Aboard the *Intrepid*, all men in CIC were killed (Combat Information Center, composed of Radar, Air Plot, and Aerology.) At noon, Renouf Russell came over from the *Massachusetts*. God, it was good to see him. He's an officer, but we lay around on the deck for a couple of hours. The *Intrepid* has had it.

December 1 Pulled out of Ulithi today. No one's in a good mood. When one accepts an island for what little it's worth, being in port can be a real comfort. For the past few days I've even relaxed. Had two liberties on Mog Mog. Am hoping to hell the carrier *San Jacinto*, or the *Bataan*, will relieve us at sea. The for'd elevator's been secured, closed down. Good! Those suicide planes (*Intrepid*) let off a gaseous smoke, and that's why so many of them died. Better check my gas mask. Have lost all enthusiam for action. In this life I want only to see home again. This time, it's January for sure. The Captain's been awarded the Navy Cross, along with two other carrier captains.

December 4 On the first, we pulled out of Ulithi with orders to soften up the Philippines. Not 3 hrs. out—you guessed it—orders were received to return to Ulithi. No one knows why, unless it's that MacArthur wants to hold off the invasion on account of rain. We'll sit around now for eight or ten days. The *Essex* has been hit by a suicide plane. Just now pulled in. I don't care for the kamikazis, not one bit.

December 10 Sandy's birthday. Age 26. Well, at long last, we're pulling out of Ulithi. Yes, it was MacArthur who decided he wasn't quite ready for Luzon. He'll have more than 400,000 men to help him out, and all his Australian reserves. The Japs won't like that. Nor I, either, who's been thinking we'd be back to the States next week, what with the elevator being secured, and all. Totally useless. It'll be like fighting with one leg up your ass. We may be relieved at sea. Come what may, this surely will be our last job before the States. Captain's inspection yesterday, but all's well. This diary was beyond reach, beyond sight, locked up in the safe, along with all the weather codes. For first time in a month, eggs and butter are now aboard. Doubt that I weigh more than 135. A package arrived from White, a book by H. L. Mencken, and cookies by Bernice.

December 15 Yesterday, began pounding Mindoro. Invaded her today, along with Mindanao, I think. No attack on us last night, and none so far today. A great blessing and a great surprise, for it means our

CAPTAIN STUART H. INGERSOLL
Commanding.
COMMANDER FRANK B. MILLER
Executive Officer

STAFF

Supervisor	P.M. Culpepper-Lt. (jg)
Editor	R.T. Winstead-PhoM. 2c
Assistant Editor	M.D. Kish——Y. 2c
Divisional Editor	A.N. Chambers——Y. 1c
Sports Editor	W.J. Coffey-AerM. 2c
Art Editor	M. James-AerM. 2c
Typist	A.V. Razukevich——Y. 2c
Chief Censor	R.H. Devenney————Lt.
	J.O. Verfaille——Y. 3c
Printers	L.T. Luther-Prtr. 3c
	E.A. Michon————S1c

Are you an OPTIMIST or a PESSIMIST?

For over a year now we have heard the optimists say, "We are going home for a rest after the next raid." and we have heard the pessimists say, "Our only chance of going home is to get a transfer". On which side of this fence are you?

"Well, I heard a fellow in the chow hall say that he heard one officer tell another that we were to be detached from the formation to go home after one more raid".

"Yeah, well, that ain't the way that I heard it because I had an officer tell me personally that he read in a confidential letter where they were going to keep the carriers out here and under the rotation of duty plan send personnel out here to relieve us when our turn comes up. And he don't give out any bum dope either. He said definitely that the ship wouldn't go back to the states until the war was over".

"Hey, did you guys hear what that radioman just said? He said that we have our orders and will be going back to the states any day now".

"Aw, that is only scuttlebutt because we are only going back to Pearl Harbor".

"I heard that the Captain was going to tell us tomorrow just what the straight dope is".

So, round and round it goes, like Major Bowes "Wheel of Fortune", and that is just about what it amounts too. "A Wheel of Fortune", for on it depends your moral and also the type of work you are going to do. You can't be working very hard if you are spending your time listening to these rumors, but whether you want to listen to them or not there is going to be someone who wants to tell them to you, and he is going to tell them whether you are listening or not. Yes, you are going to hear a lot of them. Are you going to believe the optimist or are you going to believe the pessimist? That is the question for you to decide. Will you look at the good side, and hope? Or will you look at the bad side, and give up hope? Whether the path ahead of you looks dull and dreary or sunny and bright depends on you. ARE YOU AN OPTIMIST OR A PESSIMIST?

A FEW WORDS ABOUT THIS EDITION

For the past few months there has been no "FLATTOP FLASHES" published due to the slack of interest in preparing the publications. Now that it is back on the press again, let's try to keep it there and get out an edition each month. In order to do this, we are asking the help of all hands, it is your ship's paper and it is up to you to make it the best ship's paper in the fleet. This staff that put out this edition is not permanent because the men are constantly being transferred and we are going to need new men to work on and write for the paper in order to continue it. If you are interested in this type of work during your spare time drop in and see Lt.(jg) P.M. Culpepper, R.T. Winstead, PhoM. 2/c, in the Photo Lab; or M.D. Kish, Y 2/c in the File Room.

new tactics are working: constant CAP[1] over all enemy fields, 24 hours a day of it. Soon as an enemy plane takes off, she's downed. It's really a delight—for once—to have no entertainment. Little opposition from Mindanao. Luzon will be invaded on January 9th. That's next year already. Hard to believe. Tokyo Rose says that 60 suicide planes are ready to sink the carrier *Yorktown*. She's on our port side! Unbelievably, there's still lots of talk of our returning to the States. For'd elevator still out cold. Here's hoping we retreat in a couple of days. Today our squadron, long overtime, was told by Cinpac[2] they'd not be relieved, as "your ship is returning for early overhaul." Thank God! This could mean home after Christmas. Today, the worst crash I've ever seen, plane came in, missed all barriers, and plunged into tailend of a forward plane. Big pile up. Both pilots hurt, flopped out of their cockpits, but still alive. It all happened so fast. After seeing that the descending plane would crash into the parked one, I crashed, too, for shelter, nearly killing myself diving to the catwalk. Both planes were thrown over the side. Yesterday, a torpedo wake, but the sub got away.

December 17 Yesterday, a good dogfight, but somewhere beyond the horizon. There was a time when that would have disappointed me, but we're now too near the end of the feast to risk a rotten clam. Today, reliable scuttlebutt has it that after refueling, the Captain will have an important announcement. If he says what I'm thinking, we're to be heading for Hunter's Point, Mare Island, California, on January 17th. That means we'd be immediately detached. May that be his word.

December 19 The Captain never gave that speech. Well, anyway, on the 18th we went through a great deal. A typhoon passed across us, winds up to 85 knots when the instrument broke down, and seas so high, one had to look skyward to catch their caps. On top of that, we caught on fire. All the planes on hangar deck started shifting around, and exploded, killing one man. All the planes

(opposite) Page from ship's newsletter. Drawing on right by MJ.

1. Combat Air Patrol.

2. Commander-in-Chief of the U.S. Pacific Command.

WEATHER ANALYSIS, PERIOD 16 TO 19 DEC. INCLUSIVE

On 16 December 1944 an energetic tropical disturbance was centered over the Celebes Sea southwest of Mindanao. A westerly or northerly movement of this storm was checked by a persistent and strong high pressure system bearing southward from Siberia over China extending its influence into the region of the Philippines. On the 17 th the tropical storm moved northeastward. A secondary center passed east of the ship during mid-day while the main center, increasing its intensity, was located over Mindanao. At 0400 on 18 december the typhoon was estimated to be centered about 250 miles SSW of the ship and moving NE. At 0500 the barometric reading was 1006.5 mb (29.72 inches). The condition of the sea was rough with moderate swells from the north. The wind was 013°, 30 knots. At 0700 the barometer began to fall at a moderate rate and at 0800 the barometer fell rapidly, the wind backed from 013° to 352° and increased from 30 to 47 knots, indicating the storm center would pass near and east of the ship. The barometer continued to fall very rapidly and reached the lowest reading of 975.0 mb (28.79 inches) at 1315 at which time the typhoon passed about 40 miles east of the ship. The state of sea became very high at 1100 and a precipitous state of sea continued from 1145 to 1500. From 1030 to 1500 the wind backed steadily from 360° to 242° averaging 70 - 75 knots with frequent gusts to 85 knots and occasionally to 100 knots or above. From 1500 to 1815 the wind continued to back steadily from 242° to 192° and decreased in intensity from 60 to 33 knots. The velocity decreased to 18 knots by 2030.

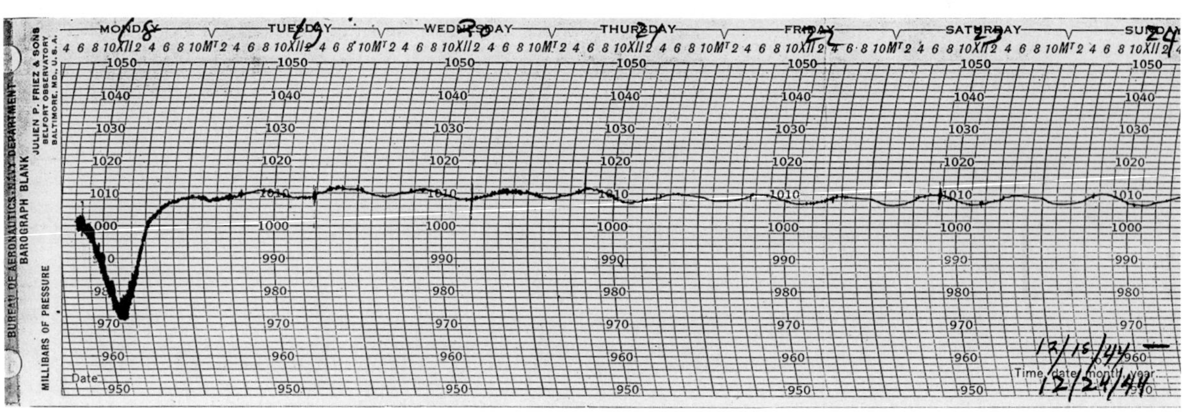

Ship's original weather analysis and barograph of typhoon.

are smashed up, ruined. Fire spread down to the next deck. A man was killed in the laundry room. Then the planes started falling off the flight deck. A man was killed there, too. We threw all the ammunition overboard, and flooded the magazine. The sides of the ship are leaking. At least 2 million bucks damage done, and damage, too, to my reputation. "How'd you let us get into *that*?" I'm asked. "Ask Halsey," I answer. The fires roared for 2 hours. Even the Captain manned a hose. So relieved we didn't have to abandon ship. No one could have survived in that sea, not for more than a minute. Two guys fell overboard on leeward side, and were at once thrown lines. Lucky. Others who fell were sucked into the depths within seconds. Nearly everything's flooded. Lots of ruination in mess halls and berthing compartments. One guy broke his back, another both arms. Others broke this and that. We lost power, too. Dead in the water 200 miles off the Philippines. A sitting duck. For protection, the task group left us with 2 cans and a cruiser. We buried our men today.

[Gerald R. Ford Library]

Damage on hangar deck caused by typhoon and fire.

[Gerald R. Ford Library]

More typhoon damage.

[Gerald R. Ford Library]

The CVLs *San Jacinto* and *Cowpens* were, also, afire. The CVE, Mr. Choun's ship, lost 44 planes. New ones, too. One can, 588, turned over, losing all but 10 men. So glad we got the fire under control. Today, all is calm, an eerie calmness, though, and it gives me the willies. We've been tossing planes overboard all day, and getting rid of water. All bulkheads black from smoke. Hangar deck completely gutted. Four planes look like beachballs. Along with the *San Jacinto* and *Cowpens*, we're going back to Ulithi, the others proceeding on to Formosa, where we were headed when so rudely interrupted. If this is what it took to return us to the States, am not sure I thoroughly approve. All too many ships damaged. Funeral was impressive. Chow really horrible now. Hours in line, too, waiting for swill. Good experience, but so tough on so many families. I'd not want to be Halsey today. Mail aboard ("Neither snow nor rain nor sleet nor..."), and a postcard from Myrtie French informing me that Philip Dupree's coming home.[1] That's nice.

December 21 Pulling into Ulithi today. Total damage: 5 million bucks. Five cans capsized, as well as several destroyer escorts. One can reports a 72 deg. roll. A great victory for the Japs.

Burial for shipmate Mauney, killed by a blast on the lower deck during typhoon.

[courtesy Frank Slater]

1. Myrtie ran French's Tavern in Dublin. Philip Dupree was her nephew.

Tall tale makes big waves

ANN LANDERS

Dear Readers:

Remember the Texan who wrote about his friend, the "champ at one-upsmanship"? The friend said that during World War II, he was on an aircraft carrier and the waves were so high they washed down the flight deck. The unconvinced Texan said, "A wave would have to be 80 feet or 100 feet high in order to do that. If you tell me there have been waves that washed over the deck of any carrier, *anywhere*, at *any* time, I'll eat my hat."

If that Texan will let me know whether he prefers mustard or ketchup, I will send him a jar or a bottle because from the looks of the mail bags piled all over my office, he is going to have to eat his hat.

Here is a sampling of the most one-sided mail I've ever read:

Dear Ann:

Here are three facts that are absolutely irrefutable:

1. Elvis is dead.
2. The pope is Catholic.
3. In a Pacific typhoon, with winds over 70 miles an hour and massive swells, waves can and will come over the top of the bow of a carrier. I've seen it happen.

JOHN M., USN RETIRED,
OXNARD, CALIF.

Thanks for the backup information. Here's more from the Department of the Navy:

Dear Miss Landers:

Enclosed you will find two photographs of the aircraft carrier USS Bennington, taken after the ship had been through a typhoon off Okinawa on June 4, 1945. I'll bet this typhoon was the one referred to by your correspondent. As you can see, the damage to the steel structural members supporting the flight deck was so massive, they simply folded over.

DAVID WALDEN,
Assistant for exploratory development,
Department of the Navy

From Albany, N.Y.: I am enclosing photos of the USS Hornet with the deck that was battered by 90-foot waves. I lived through that typhoon, and it was an experience I shall never forget.

Blaine, Minn.: I came home from Pearl Harbor submarine base on the aircraft carrier Saratoga. The sea was so rough and the waves so high, we couldn't eat at tables. We sat on the hangar deck with our backs to the bulkhead and the trays on our laps. I was also in Okinawa in 1945 during the typhoon. It was so bad, I lived for four days under a bulldozer.

Mesa, Ariz.: I hate to admit it, but that loudmouthed braggart is right. Carrier decks *can* be washed down by heavy seas. On June 9, 1945, I was in the Yellow Sea, aboard the USS Pittsburgh. The waves were more than 100 feet high, and the winds were up to 142 miles per hour.

Worcester, Mass.: In 1953, I was aboard an aircraft carrier during a NATO exercise called "Operation Mariner." The sea was so rough, the waves broke over the bow of the flight deck, and we had to cancel operations.

Clarksville, Va.: I was a 19-year-old sailor aboard the aircraft carrier USS Belleau Wood. We sailed into a typhoon that devastated Okinawa. Stars and Stripes magazine showed some great photos of this incredible happening. Unforgettable!

Sautee, Ga.: I was one of hundreds who were caught in that great typhoon 50 years ago while aboard the USS Monterey, an aircraft carrier. And by the way, there was another fellow on that carrier whose name you might recognize: Lt. Gerald Ford.

Boston Globe, May 2, 1994

President Gerald R. Ford describes his experience during the typhoon:

[from *A Time to Heal: The Autobiography of Gerald R. Ford* (New York: Harper & Row, 1979)]

'On December 18, we ran into a vicious typhoon in the Philippine Sea. Rain and hundred-knot winds whipped the ocean into a mountainous fury. That night was pure hell. I had the deck watch from midnight to four o'clock. In the pounding seas, three destroyers simply rolled over and capsized, with an enormous loss of life. At four o'clock, I left the bridge, stepped down to my cabin and tried to get some sleep before general quarters at five-fifteen.

The crew went through the predawn general quarters routine in the increasing fury of the typhoon. The wind and the rain were horrendous. I was glad when we secured, so I could hit the sack after a rough night.

I hadn't been back in my bunk many minutes before I heard the clang of general quarters again. Waking, I thought I could smell smoke. I went up the passageway and out to the catwalk on the starboard side which runs around the flight deck, where I started to climb the ladder. As I stepped on the flight deck, the ship suddenly rolled about 25 degrees. I lost my footing, fell to the deck flat on my face and started sliding toward the port side as if I were on a tobogan slide. Around the deck of every carrier is a steel ridge about two inches high. It's designed to keep the flight crews' tools from slipping overboard. Somehow, the ridge was enough to slow me. I rolled and twisted into the catwalk below. I was lucky; I could have easily gone overboard. Then, much more carefully this time, I made my way up to the bridge. That's when I realized the severity of the problems we faced. Fifteen or twenty fighters and torpedo bombers were tied on the hangar deck below. At the height of the storm, one of the planes broke loose from its cables. Every time the ship rolled, it crashed into other planes. Soon, a number of planes were darting around down there like trapped, terrified birds. Gas tanks were punctured, the friction produced sparks and a fire broke out.

Because Monterey was a converted cruiser, the hangar deck air vents were inadequate. They were supposed to funnel fresh air down to the engine and boiler rooms, but now they were funneling smoke. One sailor died of asphyxiation and 33 were injured. With no one to tend them, three of the four boilers stopped functioning. The fire on the hangar deck was raging out of control, and if we lost the boiler, we'd lose the pressure in our fire hoses and have no way to fight the blaze. We would have to abandon ship. Admirial William F. Halsey, commander of the Third Fleet, authorized us to do just that and he told two cruisers and three or four destroyers to stand by and try to rescue survivors. But our Skipper, Captain Stuart H. Ingersoll, wasn't ready to quit. "Give us more time," I heard him radio from the bridge. "I think we can solve the problem." The ship was still dead in the water. The storm was raging. The fire was uncontrolled. Ingersoll sent a rescue party wearing gas masks to the engine and boiler rooms. They brought out the survivors, kept the one boiler functioning and worked to repair the others. After seven hours of battering by monstrous waves, all our boilers were working again; we were able to extingguish the fire and steam toward the island of Saipan. Years later when I became President, I remembered that fire at the height of the typhoon and I considered it a marvelous metaphor for the ship of state.'

December 24 Few days ago, pulled into Ulithi with wounded carriers *Cowpens* and *San Jacinto*. Before the anchor was lowered, even, scuttlebutt—from beyond, from afar—had it we'd soon be landing in the States. Well, by God, we ARE! But only so because that storm crippled us out of an invasion of Luzon. Even a fool would know there's no equipment in this dump to properly repair us for further duty. Four to six months in a stateside shipyard is the prevailing opinion. I concur. We're now in process of stripping the ship, getting rid of nearly everything that one could mention in two hours, or more, like from bombs to beans. While all that's going on, we're taking aboard duds of all kinds. Duds. Why duds? Not even the stupidest shit can answer me that. It's Christmas eve.

December 30 Today, pulled out for Eniwetok and Pearl. This morning, the Captain said, "I've personal reasons to believe we'll continue eastward." I hope so. Here's hoping, also, to be granted a leave, my first ever. A kid just learned his brother had been killed at Leyte. They say he can't be consoled. Good evening, 1944, and good riddance.

Drawing by MJ, Christmas, 1944.

1945

January 10 Pulled into Pearl this morning, and though no actual orders have been received, it's a certainty we're headed for the States. Pulling out the 13th. Heading for either San Diego, Bremerton, Washington, or San Francisco. Hope it's Bremerton, because that would cut a whole day's travel time to Dublin. By bus, anyway, and that's what it looks like. It's colder in Washington, though, and they say that liberties stink. It's a dry state, and it's always raining. Maybe Frisco makes more sense. Dick Richards[1] came aboard today, and what a beautiful surprise. He popped his head in the office door, sort of peeking, and at first he didn't recognize me "for all that additional upholstry on your upper lip." I recognized him immediately. "Good God, DICK!" I cried, and everyone thought I'd lost my mind, seeing his scrambled eggs and bars. They all snapped to attention. I'll never forget it. It was almost worth the whole war. Tomorrow, will be going over to his hospital ship, the *Eldorado*. If I can find it. Will need a whaleboat to reach it. Two letters from Mum, one with a photo of Sandy, wounded, and a Purple Heart on his chest. Beautiful and sad.

January 14 Two days ago, went over to see Dick. Upon return, there was a note from a Lt. Knoderer saying that he'd run into Varick Stout,[2] and that V. would like to see me. I suppose he's a Commander, too. Getting sticky. Wrangled a special liberty. Saw him for ten minutes. Later, had one hell of a fine time with Pink Candy and Dougherty, friends from the Cape May days. Ran into them in town. They're aboard an escort carrier. Actually, Varick couldn't have been nicer. Same day, three guys from the gasoline detail got caught up in some fumes, and died. The one

1. My parents' oldest friend, Dr. Loren P. Richards.
2. Dublin friend, a summer person.

in a pipe, it took 2 days to get him out. Another casualty of the storm. That afternoon, one of our mess cooks was killed in town, by a bus, and today a guy died in sickbay, a blood clot in the brain. Looks like God's doing the Jap's work. I was having a fire watch on the hanger deck when he was brought up the ladder on a stretcher. We all stood at attention as the bugle blew. That was the extent of his funeral, at least as far as his ship is concerned. Tomorrow, we pull out for Bremerton. Will be getting second leave, bussing home with John Curtis. Will smuggle off some cigarettes for Dad. It'll be cold in the east. Dick told me, confidentially, that the next invasions (and Sandy's participation in them) will take place in that chain of islands off southern Japan, where Okinawa lies. We've already hit them, of course. Dick's is the flagship for the 4th Marines, Sandy's outfit. He says Howling Mad Smith will be aboard, and thinks Sandy may be, too. I doubt it. Just now heard that the carriers are now hitting the Japanese fleet somewhere off IndoChina. "Very daring," it says here. There was a time when I'd have felt badly missing something like that. NO MORE! Soon I must make a formal request for continued duty aboard this ship. Might as well wind my war up where it first began.

January 16 Now on way to Bremerton. The temp will be sinking to 35, a drop of some 45 degrees. Dangerous. When it's not the Japs, it's the weather. A guy went nuts the other day, and now a second barber has gone nuts. Looks like I'll be the only guy from Aerology not transferred. Payton thinks he won't be, but then, he always thinks the worst. Thinks he has tit cancer. Today, awards were given to the pilots and aircrew. Captain said that Adm. Montgomery told him he was using the *Monterey* as a example to all the big carriers, the CVs. Mostly good luck, I'd say, and that's not modesty. How we escaped without a scratch, God most surely knows, Who was our rabbit's foot. I'll be getting Second Leave: 20 days, no traveling time. Ten days at home, more or less, what with the bus, and all. There'll be no escort

Gerald Archambault, E. Butler, Nick Maselli and MJ, Bremerton, Washington.

with us from Pearl to the mainland, but who needs one? If there's a Jap between here and there, he's more to be pitied than feared. Lost. Will be pulling in near noon, Sunday the 21st. Oh glorious hour, oh happy day!

February 2 No entry for all too long, and this'll be the last of it for quite some time. Pulled into Bremerton on January 22, into drydock. Following day, the first bunch went on leave. Have come down with a cold, but also with a love for this town. Am having myself a wonderful time. Liberty every other day, and then it's off to the dives with Camera, Archie, Meyers, and Lorton. Nightclubs, women, and plenty of booze. There's a Lois Vine who'll be writing me at sea. That's her maiden name, and she's care of General Delivery. Whiskey is bootlegged. So far, it's been one big blast of remission, like a whale letting loose with its vapors. My AerM 1/c has been approved by the Bureau. In the Army, that'd be three stripes over, and two under. If Washington knew what I know, they'd have ordered my execution, instead. They're really tearing this ship apart. Around the clock. Civilians. When the clock strikes the right hour, though, it's off to Seattle I go, by ferryboat, returning by 8 the next morning. Am getting really

Berg, Pat, Gerald Archambault, MJ, Mary, Joe Camera, Ray Condon and Pat in Seattle.

Camera (far left), Archambault (far right) and MJ (center), Seattle.

unwound. Yesterday, on boarding the ship, I saluted the Duty Officer with the right leg. Automatically, he returned it with his arm, and then laughed. Everyone's unwinding. Called up Dublin, and Mum's voice sounded like a song. Will be off and away on 13th, by bus. Dana Coolidge[1] is missing in action, which means my stopping in Fall River on the long way home. Sandy's now on his way to Okinawa, south of the Ryukyus, so says Dick Richards. Danny's now in China. Well, that's it for now. Will be back for Cruise Two in the springtime. They're the suicide planes that worry me most.

[US Navy]

Kamikaze plane emerges from the fog at a sharp angle, heading for the USS *Sangamon* (CVE-26) and coming so close it took off her radio antenna. Minutes later, she took a direct hit, May 4, 1945.

1. A friend from Fall River, Massachusetts, who returned a short time later only to take his life.

[Gerald R. Ford Library]

SECOND CRUISE

March 31, 1945 to October 19, 1945

March 31 Here begins Cruise Two. Have been in Dublin, and solid heaven it was from first to last. Before leaving Bremerton, a new Aerological Officer took Choun's place, a Lieutenant Harmen. Good man. Everyone from office was transferred, save for Rachlin, their replacements being a bunch of embittered cadets (six), washed out students of flight schools. They're about as agreeable as a bunch of dead roses. They'll never be officers now, nor heroes of the sky. I'm in charge, though, and they'll just have to stomach me. They've no interest in learning codes, nor in learning anything else, for that matter. What it boils down to: it's I who's their enemy, not the Japanese. Life is more interesting, though, and I'm standing no watches. It's round-the-clock duty, a flexible life. All I do is draw maps, make forecasts, and avoid my men. A quiet war. Had a couple of days in San Francisco where I saw the Bruce Porters.[1] Wonderful few hours. We're now on our way to Pearl. There's a fresh squadron aboard. From Pearl, it's west to Japan. Sandy OK on Iwo. Survived. He was commissioned "on the field." Danny's still in Burma. Thought he was in China. The suicide planes are doing a good job, the *Monterey* about the only carrier that's not been hit. As in Cruise One, will make an entry only when there's action. Certainly, there's none in this office.

(opposite) Monterey at anchor in Ulithi Harbor (airing bedding on railing).

1. My father's sister, Peggy, and her husband.

Sandy, still a corporal, was commissioned a 2nd Lieutenant 'in the field,' on landing barge on way to Iwo Jima.

April 5 Today I missed Sandy by minutes, he rushing over to see me before taking off for Maui. He could stay but ten minutes. The guys said he looked great, handsome in his lieutenant's uniform. I must see him for sure—after the next cruise even if it means going over the hill. He'll be in the big invasion, I know. A slaughter. In his shoes, I'd walk on water—straight home. It was two days ago that we pulled into Pearl. Along with us was the *Franklin*, out but two weeks, and badly hit. Eight hundred men dead, fifteen hundred casualties, the flight deck ruined, and one whole side blown out. Terrible sight. A tough sight, too, for the greenhorns whose first time out is yet to be. Soon to pull out for pilot practice, then back for a spell. I don't look forward to the future.

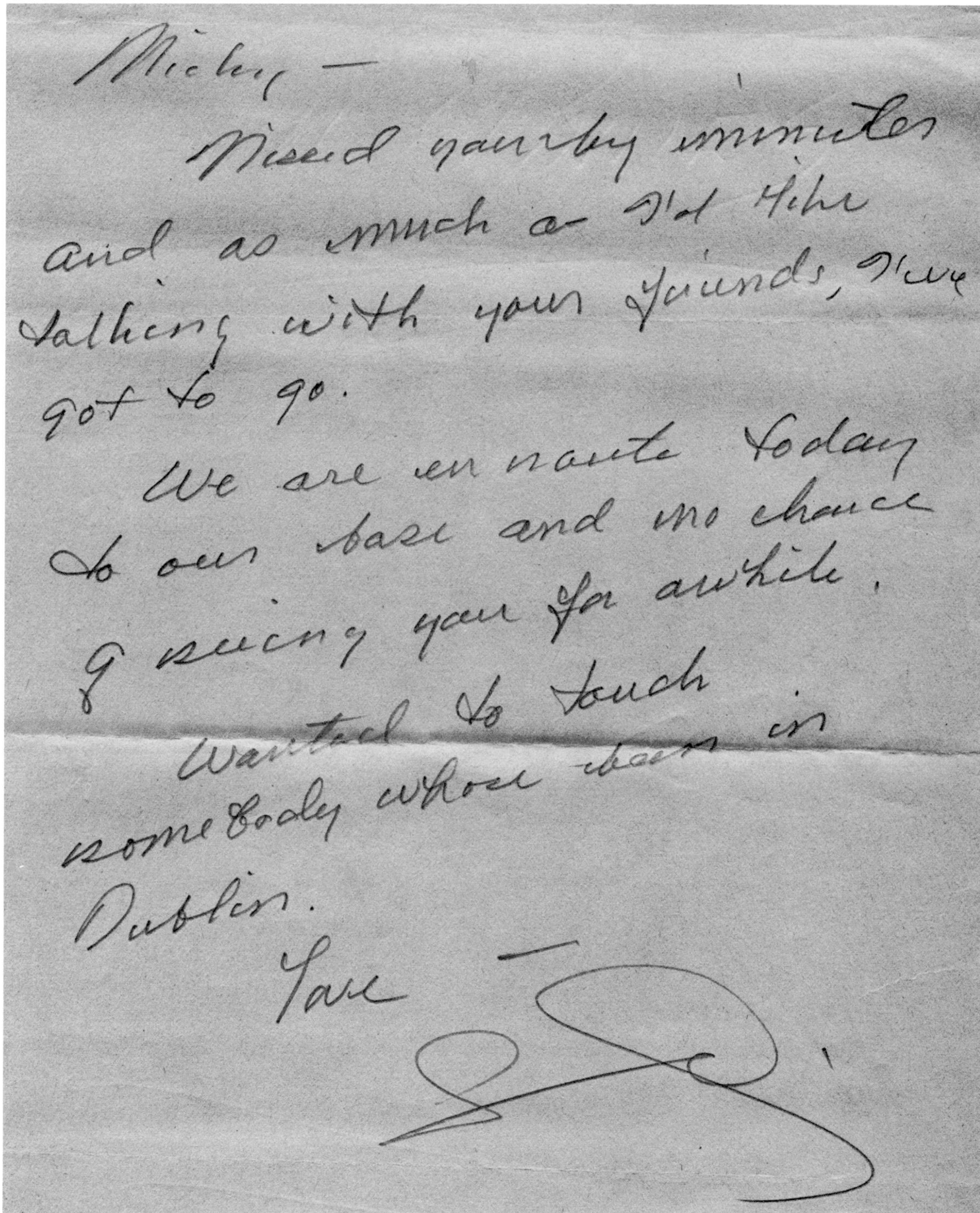

Micky, —

Missed you by minutes and as much as I'd like talking with your friends, I've got to go.

We are en route today to our base and no chance of seeing you for awhile.

Wanted to touch somebody whose been in Dublin.

Love —

S

Note from Sandy, April 5, 1945.

April 11 Pulled into Pearl today—for just what reason, I can't figure out. The sooner this war is over, the better. All's been going well, though, in the office. The cadets less bitter, though still resentful, on the whole, their dreams and pride all down in smoke. Anything requiring either mental or physical exertion is still out of the question. Now that they trust me to live without them, we all get along very well. I now sleep in the office. There's a bunk, damnit, over one of the desks, and chatter, of course, goes on day and night, around the clock. Tired as I am, it's not easy to pass out. Last night, they played catch with a helmet. Kept me awake until one of them stubbed a finger. They couldn't fly, and they can't catch, either. The Captain, damn it, wants a pre-reveille forecast, which means my getting up at 3 AM. Had hoped he'd relax. He's a nervous man, more afraid of a fog than of fire, a real nut. Am losing weight.

April 12 Today, the terrible shock. News of Roosevelt's death. Will Stalin respect Truman? Oh God, this is terrible. Tomorrow, we pull out of Pearl. More squadron practice. I say—get on with the war. This squadron's a bunch of leftovers from the *Saratoga*, the *Franklin*, and so forth. Poor Mrs. Roosevelt. This is no good at all. Nimitz announced today that the Jap suicide planes are raising hell. Even Myrtle French knows that.

April 28 Pulled out of Pearl a couple of days ago—for last time. Now headed for Ulithi. From there, who knows? Sandy says he'll soon be with us. Japan? The coast of China? The crew, both officers and men, are discontent. Lots of bitching, and all the Captain's fault. He is not a seaman. Also, the crew has premonitions, which of course is not the Captain's fault, but just the same, I don't take them lightly. The old hands, like me, are pretty sick of it all. Slowly, am training my men. Lots of psychology and patience. Rachlin's now gone, too, which means I'm the last of the original crew. Life's pretty interesting, though, in spite of it all. Soon may get flight skins. High time.

May 2 Now on our way to Eniwetok, arriving on 4th, then on to Ulithi. All hell broke loose the other night. The Japs now have a radio-controlled glider bomb. Frankly, I'm not too optimistic about any sort of a future. The kamikazi are giving the carriers hell at Okinawa, and are even diving on Ulithi. Crazy. My men demand the most patient care. Give me a Jap any day. Am now making the 36-hour forecast. Mr. Harmen and I get up at 3, he making a preliminary forecast for the day. I get the last map drawn around 10 PM. My toughest job is getting one of my bums to show up when I hit the sack. Last night, I woke up to find them switching lights off and on, signaling messages to one another. Thank God Sandy's not at Okinawa. This morning, one of our TBMs exploded in the air (in sight of ship) and plunged to the sea, one wing coming off. Pilot and crewmen lost. Operational losses aren't easy to swallow. Later, a second plane went into the drink when her tailhook snapped off after attaching itself to the arresting gear. Went over the side, just missing a bunch of gunners. By some freak of something, the motor perked up, and off she flew. Had to make a wet landing, though. Pilot got out OK. A can picked up some flesh and muscle of those three that were killed. No bones. "It" will be buried on Eniwetok. Mr. Olwell, my good friend the architect (only officer I feel free to be philosophical with), told me tonight that China will probably be invaded on the 26th of May. Hope so. Sooner the better, and the sooner home.

May 8 Yesterday, pulled into Ulithi where we took on supplies. Off early this morning. The task force has been waiting for us. In our force, 58.1, are three battleships, seven cruisers, two heavy carriers, three light carriers, and eighteen destroyers. This is the biggest task group we've ever been in, the largest, even, ever to have sailed the Pacific. Am not quite sure where we're going. China, maybe. Wherever, Sandy says he'll not be far behind. My new men will have to be more on the ball. A letter from Mum yesterday, and nine from my friend in Seattle. She really does seem to love me. I don't look forward to the future.

At anchor off Ulithi.

May 10 Yesterday, one of our TBMs lost its tail assembly, and crashed head on into the drink. Exploded. Killed all three. We're having all too many accidents this cruise. Now on our way to Okinawa. After a few days there, it's off to the Philippines, and then on to China. As far as I know, we strike somewhere around Shanghai, or however you spell it. We'll be covering for the invasion. I guess Sandy'll be there. The other night, at Eniwetok, we had what the Navy calls a "Happy Hour." We sing. Well, after the Captain appeared (he's always the last to sit down for the following movie), we sang, "Mine Eyes Have Seen the Glory of the Coming of the Lord," but with different words. It went, "The skipper shared a bottle of his whiskey with the crew, oh the skipper..." three times, concluding, "In a pig's asshole he did." Second verse: "We were only only fooling, oh we were only only fooling, yes, we were only only fooling. In a pig's asshole we were!" He up and departed. Of course, we'd never have done this to the two former skippers, Ingersoll and Hundt. Reading this, it may sound cruel, but enough's enough, and we had to let it out. His name is Lyon. Officers and men, they both dislike him. In wartime, even a saint should know something of its dirty works. Should we be hit by a storm, or by a bomb, it's the skipper's good sense, and respected command, that his ship must count on for survival. I don't think Captain Lyon is that man. Besides his stupidity, I've got to contend with my own. Some of the work around here is beyond me. That rasonde machine, for instance. Though my men are all good enough guys, and brighter than I, they're totally irresponsible. No gimp, no will. Am relied on for everything from toothpicks to typhoons. Was up this morning at 0300. We now make three forecasts a day: a preliminary one at 4 AM, one for the flagship at 11, and a 36-hour job for mid-afternoon. Sometimes, four times a day, there are upper winds to forecast for the pilots. They're for ballistics. After the first 20,000 feet, I make the rest up. Have to. What with those two maps to draw, and the caring for my grounded grouches, there's little time to think of home. Just as well, maybe. Am among the ten in V-3 Division who's on the Rotation Plan (transfer), but what I need is *immediate* relief.

May 11 Ex-cadet Seefried was relieved of mess hall duty today, replaced by washout Smith. Also, Seefried has reported to sickbay, where he may be for some time. Commander McKee, the Air Officer, wanted five men from my division to fold wings, and learning I wanted to get rid of my foundlings, he took two of them. Good. This morning the Captain said, "I'm sick of this business. Just as

Striker Seefried repairing the anemometer. At sea, a thankless and terrifying job.

[US Navy]

V-3 Division

(Top Row, l-r): O.E. Hans, P.P. Byrne, J.A. Learned, E.E. Smith, A.C. Klienpeter, G.W. Debeer, M. James, J.I. Camera, G.G. Archambault, L. Siroonian, N.J. Maselli, R.W. Hollis, O.M. Bannon, C.E. Long, S. Alman, J.M. Brown, L.B. Lowe, C.R. Swanberg, W.J. Birtwhistle, F.L. Foss. *(Middle Row, l-r)*: R.W. Elder, J.I. Fox, J.W. Herrholz, J.C. Seefried, R.E. Seckington, V.B. Garry, L.S. Bishop, E.B. Butler, G.R. Grant, R. Condon, R.W. Myers, J.C. Rogers, E.E. Lybrand, O.E. Lorton, V.L. Campodonico, H.G. Weimer, J.S. Babcock, J.E. Burke, H.H. Coshatt, Mercer. *(Front Row, l-r)*: J.R. Lewis, B.E. Thomas, Lt. Khronemeyer, Lt. Comdr. Van Maugh, Lt. Norment, Lt. Converse, Lt. J.G. Lacy, Lt. Culpepper, Lt. Floreth, Lt. Comdr. Bond, Lt. Smith, Lt. Newman, Lt. Forseythe, Ens. Jamison, Ens. Gimble, Lt. Harmen, Chief Anderson, W.E. Roth, D. Fuhrman.

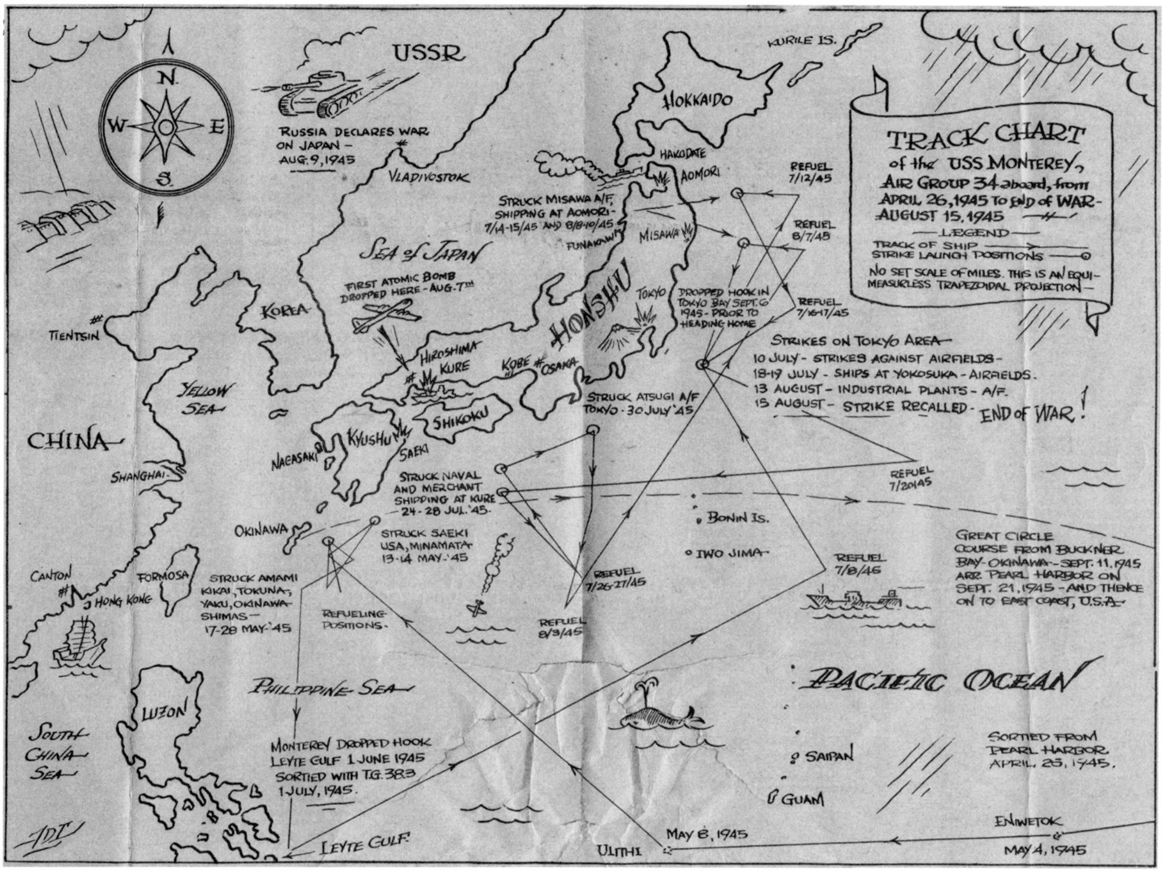

[Gerald R. Ford Library]

leave go home." Well, we're sick of *him*. Yesterday, the *Monterey* was out of formation all morning. Inexcusable. He even seeks out my opinion. That's not only unfair to Mr. Harmen, but sick, to boot. We fuel tomorrow, striking Okinawa the following day. It'll be interesting to observe the new men. Their first taste of fire. They'll enjoy it. The old hands are dreading it, their having been home and all, been all through it before. What the new hands have yet to fear are the suicide planes.

May 12 As usual, I'm all wet. We're *not* going to Okinawa. On Sunday, tomorrow, and again the next day, we hit Kyushu, the southernmost island of Japan, which is where the heart of their airforce resides. While other task groups are down at Okinawa, we (58.1) go to Kyushu—as a decoy—there to attract Jap planes, diverting them from the Okinawa operation. Our pilots don't yet know where they're going to strike. That's how indefinite it is. Their only mission is to attract Jap planes. If hitting their own in-laws back in Grand Rapids could accomplish that, that's where they'd hit. The *Monterey* has been assigned to escort any ship that gets damaged. This means we'll be slopping around at 5 and 10 knots. I don't care for that. Enemy subs will love it. Yesterday, a guy fell overboard, and the Captain cried, "Man overboard! Lower a whaleboat." My God, but that's NEVER done at sea when the ship's in formation. To his embarrassment, he soon learned better, countermanded by a subordinate. When such an emergency arises, do *anything* but alter course and speed. It's insane to suggest we stop, lower a boat, and then puttputt after some miserable gob. (Officers don't fall overboard.) That's what destroyers are for. He was picked up. This afternoon, we were detached from 58.1 to 58.3. We're now in better society. Adm. Sherman's the task group commander, a considerable improvement over Adm. Clark. Also, Adm. Mitscher's with 58.3, and he's task *force* commander. I now feel safe. Refueled today, and are now making a speed run to Kyushu. Tonight, planes from the *Enterprise* will heckle the Japs, flying over the islands at their bedtime. No sleep. They'll be mad as hell in the morning. Good. Let's make it interesting. On the one hand, am really quite leery of tomorrow, and on the other—*no*, I'm leery on both hands! Feeling this way is all quite new to me. It comes from my having been home since action last. Also, the Japs have polished up their suicide skills. Lt. Harmen is increasingly satisfactory. Good sense of humor, quiet, and easy to work with. I'd have gone nuts with Mr. Choun. More tomorrow. The other day, I got nine letters from Lois. Thought she had three kids. Make it four. And all under five. In letter no. 8, a photo was enclosed. (The whole family, minus the Mr.). Had three good times with her before leaving. Went to the Music Box.

Lt. Harmen

May 14 8:30 AM. Last night was one long GQ. Shot down a few. We lost a pilot yesterday who landed about 4,000 yards from Kyushu. Poor guy, I hope he's dead. Have just come in from a half hour of the most spectacular warfare yet. Damnit, they're suicides. Not a single bomb dropped. First off, a plane, way way up, made a dive for the *Enterprise*, the flag carrier. It was very well planned, for when all eyes were on the horizon, the guns pointing that way, too (a group of planes out there), the suicider came down unnoticed. Made a square hit. Terrible fire. Quite a sight. Then a second one dove for yet another big carrier (there's safety in smallness) and the *Monterey* nailed it. He missed. It never even had time to go up into flames. Everyone clapped. We got another one, too. Burning up as it dived, it made for a destroyer. The little can wiggled around, ducked this way and that, and escaped it by no more than the width of her bow. After that, we nailed yet a third, this one diving on *us*. God, I was scared. Was even more wound up after it *missed* us. Funny thing, I never even heard our guns. Under other conditions, like in practice firing, they can be painfully loud. The fleet, as a whole, winged a fourth, and the pilot bailed out. Lovely inferno. Now they've hightailed it for awhile. The *Enterprise* is out of commission, at least for some time. Tough. The new men are behaving much as they should—shaky, but enjoying it all. It's now an hour since peace returned and one of my men, the oldest, 31, is still shaking

[US Navy]

The USS *Enterprise* (CV-6) took a direct hit from a suicide plane.

all over. The Kyushu planes are about to land. Radar reports the first two are now coming in at 30 miles. They'll be here in 5 minutes. Incredibly, bogies are coming in, too! They may meet. I've never seen so much ackack in my life. This will suffice me for the day. Though my knees do shake, it's quite a wonderful show. Later. It's now 1 PM, and nothing's been going on for awhile. Several times, bogies at 30 miles or so, but either shot down or chased off. Skuttlebutt has it we'll be returning to Task Group 58.1 and 58.3, which have been out for quite some time. Will return to Leyte. Am at the point now where I'd like to get into the thick of it. Funny thing, that, because only 3 or 4 days ago, I dreaded this. The hell of it is, I'm a pacifist. Blame it on boredom, maybe. This morning, Merrick, the radioman who feels the same way I do, got so excited, he threw me down on the deck. By the time I got up, he was already dangling over the side trying to catch a bogie's dive from a more advantageous angle. "Hey," I yelled, "there's one diving at us on portside!" "That one's *yours*," he laughed, "mine's over here." I hope this action gives my men a sense of mission, or at least a common purpose, even if it's only to cheer me up. A washed-out pilot is a drip.

[US Navy]

A Zero takes heavy anti-aircraft fire.

[US Navy]

Enemy plane being shot down as seen from *Monterey*.

May 15 Fueling today, near Okinawa, and for first time in this war, re-arming at sea. This is Nimitz's bright idea, which he calls his "Floating Hotel" strategy. Food will be delivered, too. This way, a ship can remain at sea for days on end. Forever, even. Though this means we'll not be hitting port for some time, am all for it. Get the war done, I say. We used to be out for 10 days or so, make a 2-day strike, and return to port for food and fuel. Yesterday, 5 planes were shot down. The log on the bridge credits the *Monterey* with two of them, and with two assists. Hope there'll be some mail today. Later. No mail, but Nimitz's Hotel is quite something. Floating around out there is an ammunition ship, a hospital ship (Dick Richards on it, maybe), a food ship, a supply ship, and various tankers. Hospital ship taking on guys from the *Enterprise*. Following message overheard, Nimitz to another ship: "I know you've navy nurses on that ship, but get the hell back in formation!" No time today to re-arm. No one knows where we go from here, and 600 miles NE there's a typhoon taking shape. Don't think it'll bother us, though. They say there's 250 bags of mail for the task group. That'd mean 6 or 8 of them for us. Poor dad and mum.

May 16 Last night, three British ships sailed smack through center of our formation. "We didn't get you on our radar," they explained, which means they somehow missed 32 ships! "Tell the Captain we're dreadfully sorry." I wonder how "Captain" Mark Mitscher liked *that* demotion! Rearming today. So far, I've had 15 fillings. Good dentist. I've soft teeth, particularly vulnerable to this non-calcium diet of ours. It's when the ship's pitching that I dread the drill. Cancelled the last appointment. Rough weather.

May 18 Yesterday, hit the Ryuku's, and again today. We now occupy nine-tenths of the island. Got sight of a secret dispatch this morning that says we'll be around here till the 24th. Mail taken off today, first time at sea. Bogies around, but no attack.

May 19 Today, will fuel, rearm, and pick up provisions, compliments of three specific ships. While this idea of Floating Ships will speed up the war, it also means we'll be out for days and days and days. Am doing the forecasts quite often now, mostly by lettered intuition. At 1500, a fleet forecast is made, and three hours later, one for the night and following day.

May 26 All's been pretty quiet for the past few days. A few GQs, of course, but always the bogies are shot down out of range of the force. Dull. Yesterday, the interpreter on the flagship picked up a Jap message stating that starting at 0916, there'd be the first of ten suicide raids. That was their order-of-the-day, and that was that. Couldn't, as it rained all day. (I bet they could have killed themselves!) At 0900, we went to GQ with bogies at 7 miles, and all were shot down before reaching target. Had it been clear, we'd have had a big time of it. To Leyte on the 27th. They almost made me a Duty PO, but I wrote a letter to Lt. Comdr. Davis. Also argued with the Division Officer. Got out of it. Said it'd be too big a load to carry, what with my vigorous schedule, and all. That wasn't quite the truth, though, for I could easily have carried it out. What I *didn't* say was that I'd rather do the work myself than tell others what to do. I don't care for power. Much relieved. Have been depressed lately. I've the rotten suspicion that all my old friends like Camera, Archie, Burke, Masselli, Condon, Mahoney, etc., are soon to be transferred. Will feel like a stranger in my own damned house. My Seattle Lois is definitely trying to convince me that I'd be a good father to her 4 little kids. Writes every day. Asks me to picture them sitting by a fire all cozy and warm. "Oh how you'd love them!" she writes in today's. "I sit here tonight, and I'm thinking of you." The other day, sent a picture of them, but one's missing. If she doesn't cool down, I'll be missing, too.

Lois

May 27 Tonight, or late this afternoon, we received a desperate plea from Okinawa asking us for God's sake to send them some air support. Our planes are over there right now, and it's now 7 PM. Maybe we're landing more troops. Who knows? The Captain tells us nothing. The ship has been dodging mines, now for 3 or 4 days. They're everywhere. Destroyers blow them up. A sub nearly got a can today. Long days. For first time in my life, have fallen asleep in a chair. Am quite proud of that, for it shows I've learned to relax. If that's what combat can do for me, fine. Fairly sure we're going to Leyte, and I look forward to that. Want to get roaring drunk.

May 28 We *were* on our way to Leyte, but then Halsey suddenly took over, and the Fifth Fleet became Halsey's Third Fleet. We may yet go to Leyte, but right now our course is 050. Though we get there by way of Okinawa, I've the stinking suspicion, if he's the same ol' Bull, we continue on to Japan! Goodbye, drunk. Last night, blew up 3 mines. Would hate to get caught below decks. Don't know what's the story on the Rotation Plan transfers. Also, am confused as to just what I really do want when all the old faces disappear. Would be lonesome as hell, but if I did quit the ship, I know damned well I'd get restless again. Could stomach no more Cape Mays, not after all this. Mail yesterday, and more today. We're now opposite Okinawa. Several GQs lately, this morning's before reveille, but all bogies were either shot down or chased away. Not a one reached the force.

June 2 Yesterday, pulled into Leyte. Liberty consists of 2 beers and a ditch. Will hang around here for ten days, then beat it. We're loading on cold weather gear, which means the Kuriles, Northern Japan, or some such other chilly place. Today, Harmen goes over to Weather Central where he'll try to transfer 4 of the men. I wish him success. It'll mean more work, of course, but the atmosphere will be cleaned. Among them, only Seefried has recovered from washing out of flight training. He's actually learning the codes.

June 8 It doesn't look as though those 4 men can be transferred. Disappointing. Just being in Leyte, though, may be more than I deserve. A plane, yesterday, lost control and dove into the big carrier *Randolph,* to our starboard.

June 11 Tomorrow, going over to Tacloban with Mr. Harmen and Merrick. Am a lucky guy, because without the Captain's permission, no one's allowed to go inland. We'll be picking up helium tanks for the weather balloons. We've had a typhoon. Am afraid Halsey may have run into the thing.

June 12 Today, Merrick and I went to Tacloban, the capital of Leyte, and to Tolosa, too, where the Weather Central is located. What a day! Best one of the war. No one would want to go a second time, though. Tacloban is not a town, but a drainage system. Filthy is too polite a word for the place. Tolosa, not being the capitol and all, was, of course, even more stinking. City Hall,

Signpost at crossroads on Leyte, put up by homesick GIs.

[US Coast Guard]

and a house where MacArthur lived for awhile, are the two only genuine buildings in town. The others are one-room shanties on stilts. Whole families live in these, their lives an open book. Less privacy, even, than on the *Monterey*. The generations seem to be enjoying themselves, though, especially the kids, who are naked. Well, not just the kids. Saw a middle-aged woman—completely nude—as we walked by her shack down a muddy road bordered by drainage systems that stank to high hell. I nodded, but she had the grace to wave. Felt pretty small. No terlets, of course, and no running water, either. Also, there was no place to eat—because the restaurants, which sell only whiskey and buns, were out of bounds, being so dirty and all. One man wanted my shoes for two parrots. Gave him my raincoat, instead, in exchange for a wad of Japanese invasion bills. We hitched 20 miles to Tolosa, and on way back, between rides, visited a family of three generations, all in one room. On stilts. The grandmother was chopping up a chicken, on the floor, where the whole gang sleeps. There's a rumor that we pull out tomorrow, though I doubt it.

June 20 Pulled out today for some gunnery practice. Yesterday, at Tolosa, there was a meeting of all Third Fleet Aerological Officers and senior men in aerology. It couldn't have been less interesting, though I did have a fine time. Mr. Harmen got me some beer, and I got myself a haircut and 9 packs of gum. Returned to ship with half the beer, which I gave away, as well as most of those Japanese bills. Half the gum, too. Why I did this, I don't know. Not like me. In the old days, I was a hoarder, gave away nothing, even collected interest on loans. Even so, there are 5 beers in my locker to be enjoyed some day. Come to think of it, I guess that's hoarding! Well anyway, I'm less greedy. Only in Leyte could one make it safely aboard with booze. No officer-of-the-deck around. Still don't know where we head from here. Been here a long time. Am contented, though. Yesterday, Buckner was killed on Okinawa.

July 2 Have pulled out of Leyte for a month's cruise. Unhappy to depart. We'll have some targets in the Tokyo area. After that, we'll head for the Kuriles. We've been joined by a British task force of 4 carriers and whatnot. Striker Van Gilder's been transferred to the *Bataan*, and Clark to the *Essex*. Everything's going more smoothly these days. I enjoyed Leyte so much, what with its beach and sleeping till five. This getting up at 2 every morning could be a greater threat to my life than the Japanese. There's a chance I'll be making some weather hops. Good.

July 5 These early hours, and no further sleep, it's getting me down. Am sure that even the Japs get some sleep in the afternoons. In PM, before showertime, I try to crap out for an hour—behind the rasonde machine—but that's not always so easy. Often, someone else is hiding out there. At times, the body actually aches from fatigue. I now weigh 130. We're on our way to Tokyo. Should be there by the 10th. No idea how long we'll hang around. We'll have some B-29s, thank God. Even so, it'll be pretty rough. Am sick of all this. We'll be within 60 miles of the mainland. Battlewagons will bombard the coast at night from a distance of 10 miles. The British carriers will give the Japs additional targets to pick on. That's good.

July 6 Seems that this task group will fly off a weather hop every four days, one from each carrier. Mr. Harmen and I will alternate. He went yesterday, and I'll go on the 9th, my 22nd birthday. It'll be my first carrier takeoff. Zzzooom! Will be in gunner's seat. Actually, my mind's more in it than my heart. So near Tokyo and all, would rather go sledding. We hit Japan in four days. Here's hoping there'll be no snoopers on the 9th. If tactically possible, we'll hang around Japan for a week. If still afloat, it's then back to Leyte.

July 7 Yesterday, we had a two hour fire, starting down in the aft fireroom. It got pretty bad. The Executive Officer passed out. Good. No explosions. Today, a guy got his face in a propeller. Has a 50/50 chance. All goes well. Am thinking of sleeping down below. Less confusion than in office, and earlier to bed. It's a matter of not wasting away. We hit Japan on the 10th. Been a long time acomin'.

July 9 My birthday, and the weather hop's been scrubbed. Maybe just as well. Could have been the Japs who blew out my candles.

July 11 Hit the Tokyo area yesterday. Lost 4 TBMs. Rescued all crews save one. Subs picked them up five miles from Japan, in Tokyo Bay. No enemy planes got to us, though 8 or 10 were shot down from afar. Opposition surprisingly light. My weather hop was cancelled in order to give the pilot some rest. That's OK, because I needed some, too. We're now on our way to fuel. Will strike northern Japan in a couple of days.

July 13 Today, we're supposed to hit the northernmost island of the empire, Hokkaido, but the weather's so bad, all operations have been cancelled. We're now milling around, and that's not all that healthy. Too damned many mines in the waters, and subs.

July 19 Been hitting the Tokyo area for now about one week, and incredibly, no opposition save for those first few days when 3 or 4 planes were shot down on their way to see us. Absolutely no opposition. Only answer can be that they're saving it all for Sandy's invasion. The weather's been stinking. One day we had to dump bombs into the sea, the planes did, so low was the overcast. Apparently, a plane mustn't land with its belly full of bombs. Funny thing, after all this time, it was only just now that I learned that. For two days, we just milled around—off Tokyo, all operations cancelled. My weather hop has never happened.

July 23 The papers are certainly playing up the war out here. Tough on parents and wives. We're now able to hang out indefinitely. For past 2 or 3 days, the fleet's been rearming, refueling, and rebeaning (rice and beans—day after day). For first time, the "darken ship" rule has been lifted, permitting lights topside. Quite a sight to see the ocean all atwinkle with bulbs, and so close to Japan! After taking on supplies, though, they all went off. The black sea returned. This afternoon, a sub was sunk right plumb within our formation. She should have got us when the lights were on. Also, a mine was blown up. Tomorrow, we're going to strike Kobe, Japan. Also, we've sighted remnants of their fleet. Will be out here till the 8th, they say. I may be transferred when next we hit land. Am of a mind to buck such an order. Yesterday, a letter from White who's going to have a kid. Bernice, that is. If a boy, will be named Michael James. Am touched. Says his wife, who's never met me, of course, "Well, anyway, it's a good Catholic name." Am now sleeping belowdecks again. Means more sleep. If torpedoed, though, it could mean a permanent sleep. Mail has arrived. Lois unhappy. One from Sandy, and THREE from Mum!

July 24 Hit Kobe today. Sank a cruiser, and damaged a battlewagon and a couple of carriers. Though all results not in yet, on radio I heard a newsman say "Halsey's Third Fleet is at this moment striking Kobe." He may know more than I do. We've just this minute been attacked. A small one, though. Two suicide planes were shot down, one landing within the formation. Will cope again with Kobe in the morning. It's all quiet now, and in the dead of night. Am thinking we'll see no real action until the invasion, as they're saving everything for that. What about Sandy, I wonder?

July 31 Been hitting the Tokyo area now for a week. Little air opposition. Lately, only eight have been splashed within eyesight. I'm a pacifist, but this is just plain boring. The Japanese have refused our peace terms. Have a feeling I'll be transferred when next in port. Hardly think I wish to be. Besides missing out on the final act, I'd miss lots of good friends. Funny thing, though, no one is ever missed for very long. It's not like losing a dog. Also, I don't look forward to the redeployment of body and soul. A station in the States might require too much of my weary mind.

Am like an old man, too old for change. Besides, am sick of the whole damned business. Am now getting up every morning at midnight. Will hit Korea tomorrow, and retire on the 8th, next week. Port by the 15th. And what after that? Why, Japan, that's what. The big push, the invasion. Am looking forward to that in a morbid sort of way.

August 4 Were supposed to have struck Korea on the 1st, but because of a typhoon that's been in the way, we've been ducking this way and that for four days. It's now over Korea. Tomorrow, will hit Kyushu, instead. Should be out for another two weeks, our longest bout yet. Am half expecting a transfer, and have half a mind to refuse it. Am thin as hell. My nickname is "Slim." Feel well, though, and exercising afternoons with a "medicine ball" (weighs about 25 pounds), throwing it—hard as one can—from one guy to another, each about four feet apart, catching the thing on the belly. Though thin, am hard as nails. At long last, a letter from Danny, who writes I'll hear from him again "when the next Messiah joins the United Nations." Sounds himself, thank God. Am drawing flight pay this month. Have over $400 on the books.

Task Force 38 of Halsey's Third Fleet maneuvers off Japan.

[US Navy]

August 8 Today, and at long last, we're making a strike. Been milling around doing nothing for over a week. The other day we were having dive bombing practice (planes diving on the fleet) when a TBM (crew of three) twisted off its hind end, splintering it all over the place, and plunging headlong into the sea, just missing a carrier. Its crew had little more than ten seconds to give their bum luck any thought. Tough to behold, and it made my stomach ache. For some time, pieces of the plane continued floating down to the sea. The other day, I had the pleasure of being told there wasn't a man in the division who'd not give me the shirt off his back. If true, it's because I'm the least officious petty officer 1/c they've ever encountered. "Democratic," he called me. It's true I go out of my way to swab with the seamen, but that's because I love the exercise. Also, I don't care to give orders to the lowly. Most of them have been busted for one reason or another. Then, too, I'm polite. We strike Hokkaido today, then back to port.

August 10 Yesterday, we attacked northern Honshu, and again today. Yesterday, Russia declared war on Japan. We're now using an atomic bomb. It looks good. I do hope the Japs will quit. Yesterday, they gave us a little action for first time in days. A can took on a suicide plane. Five were shot down. Today, we expect the works. I don't like it, not at this late hour of the game. A guy's just been killed by a propeller. He lived six hours. His right hand was stuck on the wing of another plane, and the pilot refused to take off until it was removed. We'll bury him this morning. Am getting fed up, getting up every night before midnight. This bomb could be more than they say it is. Flattened a whole town. Russia may know something I don't. Am expecting a transfer. Hope the war's over before going home again. Today's the 41st consecutive day at sea, the longest stretch ever. Am looking forward to port. This atomic thing is unbelievable. Just now heard it has the force of the sun. I don't get it. It's hard to get it all into one's head. Anyway, here's hoping it ends the war before Sandy tanks it into Japan. I don't approve of Russia's entry now that we've practically horizontaled Japan, though right now will accept anything that works. This atomic bomb is Buck Rogers stuff, pure and simple. Our ace card.

August 13 Two nights ago, late, and after all day near the radio, three guys came below, woke me up, and said, "The war's over." As long as I live, will never forget the next 20 minutes. Though half asleep, I knew deep down they weren't kidding. "No, no, NO!" I cried, and flew out of the sack to wake up the others. We all almost bawled. Then the lights went on, and everyone stumbled around half crazy, shaking hands. There were some who just said, "Fuck off," and went back to sleep. It was terribly moving. There's a typhoon to the north. We're ducking it. Halsey wants to remain off Japan so that when the final word's to be heard, he can sail into Tokyo Bay toot-tooting his battlewagon, and sporting his scrambled-egg baseball cap. Actually, am not so sure they've surrendered yet. Somehow I feel so sorry for them all. Each ship will release ten percent of her crew to serve as an occupation force. I'd rather occupy a den of porcupines. They'll be called "volunteers." That's not for me. Not out from the fry pan to a fire. Sorry. I sure hope we'll accept their condition that the Emperor remain, and that they'll accept ours that he may, though only if we can use him. This must end now. For some reason, we still have a strike scheduled for tomorrow. It's now midnight, and we're waiting for Truman to give the word. He's scheduled to speak at any time. Today's strike has just now been cancelled. Wouldn't have blamed the pilots had they strafed at 60,000 feet. It's amusing to see the Invasion Volunteers training on the flight deck. Most of them have never held a gun. Small arms. When they're not aiming at whitecaps, they're zeroing in on the bridge—when the Captain's back is turned. Here we are on the brink of victory, yet desperately learning how to hold a gun! Well, it's now tomorrow, and we're still expecting the word. I've a stinking suspicion carriers won't be invited to Tokyo Bay. Only the bombardment ships. Today, the British carrier, *King George*,

Pistol practice after the war is over.

[US Navy]

Victory flag flies on Armitice Day.

is joining our force. It's now 5 PM of the 14th, and damn it, that strike that was cancelled took off at dawn. Been hitting Tokyo all day. Our force shot down 10 planes today, and Truman's supposed to speak at midnight, our time. We've heard that before. We've instructions to haul out our flags. Didn't know we had any. They're called "battle flags." Also "personal flags," whatever they can be. Our skivvies, maybe. We've also orders to follow all movements of the flagship *Missouri*.

August 15 Yesterday, the good word that the Japanese had agreed to quit. More rejoicing and handshakes. Emotions spilled. It's now 2:30 in the morning, and the word's come in from D.C. that Japan's message omits what the world's been longing to hear. For first time in this war, I'm really annoyed. We'll strike Tokyo again today. The Invasion boys are all set to go. Learning to shoot on Armistice Day! There's no sugar aboard, nor meat and potatoes. One slice of bread per meal. Nothing left but carrots and rice. Even the beans have gone. Right now, there's not enough food for chopsticks, even. The sweet taste of victory! While the two sides bicker, Halsey will float around, around 300 miles from the mainland, if necessary, for weeks. So here's to no food at all. Been out now for 46 days. Christ, I hope Sando won't have to invade the place. Back again, and it's now 9 AM, and the Japs have surrendered. Sando will live, and Danny, perhaps. Me, too. All afternoon, though, they've been attacking us. A portside carrier was attacked by a suicide plane. Shot it down. Five or six others were knocked out, too. Desperate men, poor souls. Halsey spoke to the fleet this PM. Now flying our big flag. The Captain's not yet said a word. He won't, either. Dullest man I ever met. No imagination.

August 18 Still steaming around Japan, hoping to land our Volunteers. Maybe tomorrow. MacArthur's the big shot, not Halsey. The food's almost out. What little bread there is, is full of bugs. Sando should be mustered out soon. Don't know about Dan. I'll be in for a year at least. Peacetime Navy is strictly shit. Scuttlebutt has it we'll return to the States in October.

August 20 Looks like we'll be out another three weeks, which would break the previous record for duration at sea. Already it's 50 days. Halsey's supply ships notwithstanding, the food is simply terrible. Milk's given out, as well. The fruits of victory! After the war, Joe Camera and Nick Maselli are going to get me over to Rhode Island for a big spaghetti.[1] Many of the Volunteers and *all* the Marines took off today. The danger is—they're now *drafting* volunteers. Doubt that they'll be needing aerographers. As air support, we'll be laying off Kyushu for awhile, along with the *Ticonderoga* and *Bataan*, plus a few cans. No mail from home.

August 23 Every plane in Third Fleet flew overhead today for their portrait. Twelve hundred, more or less. Will hang around here for another two weeks. Believe I'll go down to the Exec.'s with request for continued duty. Having walked this far, a new shoe would pinch.

August 29 Yesterday, Halsey sailed into Tokyo Bay. We've been patrolling around Kyushu now for a week. Soon it'll be 60 days at sea. Meals reduced to one piece of bread and a few little beans. Yesterday, a General Alarm sounded in the afternoon, and we all

1. Invitation honored, May '46.

Third Fleet flies in formation over Tokyo Bay.

got hell for *walking* to our battle stations. Turned out we knew better than to break our necks: a friendly plane.

August 31 Will be out until at least the 15th (seventy-six days at sea). The States by October, though! The Point System has been revised in sea duty's favor.[1] That'll give me an additional 10, which adds up to 38. When the battle stars are included, I'll have 44, and my discharge. Must cut down on smoking. Truman most satisfactory.

September 5 We've now been out for 66 days. It's a few minutes after midnight, and moments ago, the *Bataan* and *Monterey* were detached from the group, and are now on our own, heading for Okinawa. Why there, I don't know. Yesterday, a message came in asking if we were prepared to take on some 500 American prisoners (ex), to deposit, maybe, in Manila, Pearl, or possibly the States. Fearing what could happen should we hit the States, asked the Personnel Officer to bestow me permanent duty until such time as my release. "Why not?" he said. Censorship regulations have been abolished. A pilot just told me we're going to Okinawa, and then on to Pearl. I've 477 bucks on the books. Am wondering about Dan and Sando. When will we all be home?

1. Number of earned points determined time of release.

This was the 10,000th landing on the flight deck of *Monterey*, September 3, 1945.

September 6 We *were* going to Okinawa. At midnight, orders came to beat it back to the task group now heading for Tokyo Bay. The Navy's just like an ol' bat, always changing her mind. We've speeded up to 20 knots. Later. It's now 3 in the morning, and there she is, the *Ticonderoga*! Never thought I'd see her again. At 9 this AM we'll be in Tokyo Bay. Been 66 days at sea. A record. After picking up prisoners (ex), we'll proceed to Pearl, dump them there, and then shoot for the EAST COAST, where we'll decommission the ship. That's the rumor. If true, then I'll have been aboard this ship from her commissioning to decommissioning. We'll all be kicked off. Weighed myself in the butcher shop. 128 pounds. Have lost 14 since the States—last March. Good God, I just saw Japan!

September 8 Tokyo Bay looked like any other bay. Mt. Fujiama was with her usual cap of snow. We're now out to sea. Pulled out of the Bay after 5 lousy hours. Irritating, so brief a call, having gone out of my way these past 3 years—to get there. It's been from Kavieng to Tokyo! From Cape May to today, and now on my sweet way home! Will pick up some guys in Okinawa. If they're released prisoners, we'll have to give up our sacks. Am not telling mum and dad I'm coming home. Simply said I might make it by

Thanksgiving. Believe we'll pull into Brooklyn Navy Yard around the 27th of October, which is Navy Day. Dread contemplating a transfer. I've now 478 bucks on the books. This East Coast landing cuts out cross country expenses, but if I'm to continue lending money as I have in the past, I won't even have bus fare to Times Square. Wrote H.J. that should we dock in Brooklyn, it's at his place, not mine, where we should meet again. I mean, it's off to Yap I swim if I see him on the dock. He'd bewilder my friends. Tojo was never the problem Uncle Harry could be. Movies on the hanger deck now, and no GQs in the mornings. Food still terrible. Half rations, too. (A kindness, maybe.) In wartime, they'd never have let it come to this. "Nothing too good for the boys" was the word. I hunger for the good ol' days.

September 10 Have pulled into Okinawa. We've some 400 passengers aboard, *not* prisoners, though, so no one's losing his sack. They'll sleep on the deck. Pulling out this evening for Pearl, a week or 10 days haul. Back when we were in the States, we brought two pints aboard, stowing them away for a celebration at a later time. Have had 8 beers in my locker for about 3 months, to use as chasers. The pints were hidden by some Radar guys. Last night, six of us decided it was time (no one thought of it when peace was declared), and not having drunk for so long, and having lost so many pounds, and its being on an empty stomach and all, it sure worked fast. By midnight, was completely stewed. One hell of a fine time. I commend the guys who had the pints. It's quite something to be out so long without giving in to temptation. Also, they could have been sold for 50 bucks each. Minimum.

September 17 Hit Pearl a few days ago, pulling out next week, and then it's off for the Panama Canal. The Air Department, which includes Aerology, will be restricted here (no liberties), unless we pass a strict field day on Thursday. Goddamned Captain! Am to give a lecture to the Division this PM, on Aerology. Hope to make them laugh. Am hoping, also, that Danny and Sandy are home when I'm there. No news from Dublin since before the armistice. Ship to be decommissioned in Brooklyn. Hope to get a 30-day leave. Just now crossed the International Dateline, and for the *last time*, by God.

September 27 Pulled out of Pearl on the morning of the 25th. Had two great liberties there with Meyers and Lorton. Stuffed ourselves at the "Steaks and Chops," whiskey sours at the "Tropics," and then a couple of hours on Waikiki Beach, raising hell. Bought $5.50 worth of provisions. Volunteered for a working party the other day, loading stores, and smuggled 8 cans of apricots, 3 big tins of applesauce, 5 packages of grapenuts, and some peaches. A good haul. Unless the inspection parties are actually *looking* for something, there's no danger of discovery. Have been hungry now for three months, and am damned if I be so on way home. We hit Panama on the 8th, there for 4 or 5 days. Mum will come to New York for Navy Day! She'll see us parked on the Hudson. Every day now it's chip chip paint, sprucing up the ship for retirement.

October 13 Panama exceeded expectations. Got lots out of my system, beginning with the stomach. Upchucked. Went to the Monte Carlo with Condon, Meyers, Bannon and Lorton. We all got looped. Had shore patrol for a couple of days, eight hours a day.

MJ, Bob Myers, Ray Condon, Mike Bannon and Orlan Lorton, Panama.

Second day was the best. My beat was a couple of restricted whorehouse districts. They fed me both meals (outside), invited me in for ice tea and beer, cookies, too, but I declined. Restricted, they were, because they'd not been inspected. They have 2 and 3 room apartments, but carry on most of the business at home. Wonderful day. We're now on our way to New York. Navy Day's on the 27th. Dan is home, and Sando on his way. Mum and Dan will probably go to N.Y. We'll dock at Greenwich Village. Good. And here's hoping to remain aboard.

October 19 Pulled into New York, Pier 26. For some reason, the Statue of Liberty left me without emotions. Not the skyline, though, for I knew that Uncle Harry was somewhere out there. He and Doro

[US Navy]

Docked in New York and waving to waves.

will be driven to the ship by their chauffeur. Ouch. Few people were here to greet our arrival, mooring, as we did, at 0600. We're here till Navy Day, then over to the Brooklyn Navy Yard. We leave for Europe on November 14th, to return with U.S. troops. On voyage over, we'll have Italian prisoners aboard. Doubt there'll be time for a leave. Very disappointing. Liberty last night, and wound up at a dance hall in the Bronx. Upstairs. Sang a duet with a talented songstress, which ended up my singing all alone. She gave up. Too much laughter. It was "Alice Blue Gown" that we sang. I knew only the first line, and that's why it turned into a rout. The five of us picked up 6 girls. Went to a night-club. Boarded the ship at 5 AM. Pooped today. Am calling home every day. Have spoken to Sandy, not Danny yet. Haven't seen the H.J.'s yet. Ticklish. Sure as hell they'll want to see the ship. I mean, *board* her. Mum and Dan will be here on the 26th. I parade tomorrow. Visitors are swarming all over the ship. Will be out of this outfit by Feb.

October 22 Next week, it's to Brooklyn, and mid-November, it's off to Le Havre, where U.S. troops will come on. Yesterday, was in the bus, all set to parade down Sixth Avenue, when I was handed a Special Delivery from Mum. Dad sick. Told the commander, and he let me out. Took the train to Greenfield, where I was met by a thinner, more sober Danny. Stayed home until Sunday. Sandy was there, too, ready to be mustered out. It was the five of us together for the first time in five years. Dad looked a lot older. Angina. Will always treasure those few days. Got back to New York at 4 this morning, walking the streets till 7. Tim Pickering's[1] stationed here, and wants all his liberties with me. Not possible. All tied up in Brooklyn. Three days ago, Uncle Harry and Doro came aboard. H. hurt at my not seeing them. Was tied up. Will go see them on the 25th. Mum arrives Friday, when Agnes deMille will take us to "Oklahoma!". New York will be just great when some of these social obligations are behind me. I prefer Brooklyn and the Bronx. That's where we have the good times.

---

1. Reverend Timothy Pickering was a classmate at Pomfret School.

Crew standing at attention (Hudson River), waiting for Truman to sail by.

Truman.

October 27 Navy Day today, and a good thing it isn't Navy *Week*. Cold as hell, lined up for hours on the flight deck waiting for Truman to salute us. He didn't, but that's because *we* didn't salute him, either. Were the only ship among 40 or so that failed to fire those 21 shots. Captain Lyon never gave the order. The man's no sailor even at anchor. My God, even the subs fired. They say we'll now not be issued the Presidential ribbon. Truman was on a can, standing very straight, waving to the people on Riverside Drive. We put up with all those freezing hours just to be ignored, embarrassed, robbed, and despised. "Oklahoma!" was good fun. Maybe I'll get a 7-day leave.

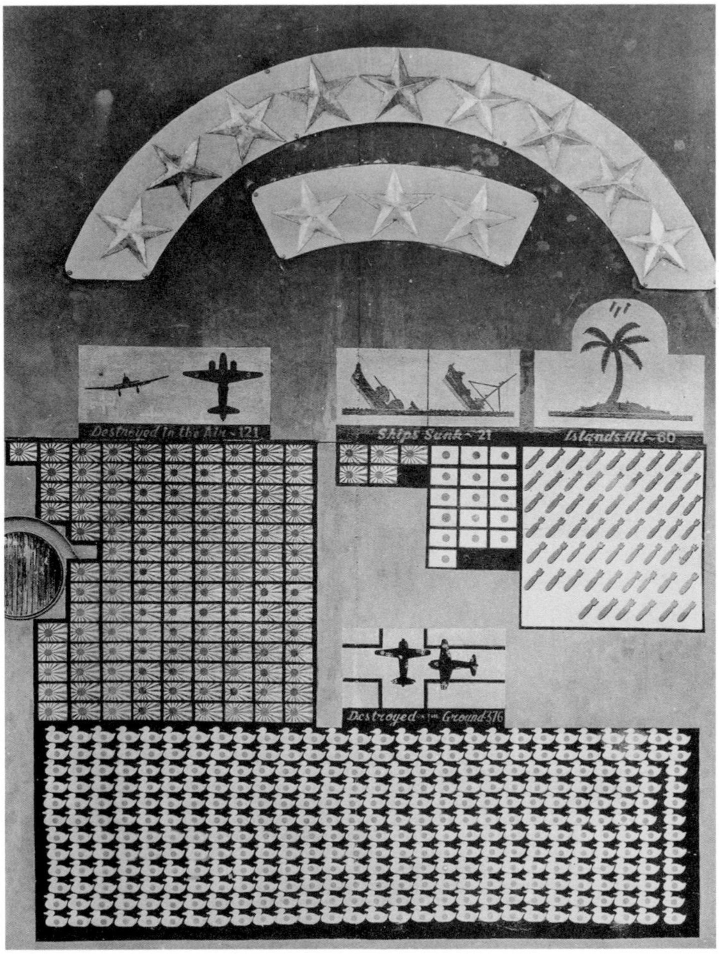

Our score board for the war: 11 naval battles, 21 ships sunk, 60 islands bombed, 300 shore targets, 500 Jap planes destroyed on the ground.

Butler, Archambault, Condon.

Waiting around for pistol practice.

Grant, Butler and Meyers, Richmond.

Moments before friends depart. I was only one not transferred.

Friends on way to new assignments.

[courtesy William E. Terheun]

Bill Terheun after surgical technique training, 1943.

Roth and Garry, en route to Italy.

MJ in New York.

[courtesy Frank Slater]

Photographer's Mate Frank Slater with aerial recon camera.

[courtesy Sig Alman]

(Back row, l-r) V. Garry, Ned Bishop, Jack Learned, Bill Grant. *(Front row, l-r)* Bob Meyers, John Seefried, E. Smith, W. Roth, Sig Alman.

Friends aboard whaleboat *(above)*. MJ sees them off *(right)*.

Friends from Air Plot, Radar Plot and Aerology, were all transferred, leaving me *(first row on right)* responsible for all weather forecasts.

John Seefried, my only help in the aerological office, was later to become a parson.

Keeping a close eye on the weather.

THIRD CRUISE

November 18, 1945 to 3 pm, January 1, 1946

November 18 It's now 3 weeks since an entry, and all this time it's been in New York, mostly Times Square and the Bronx, and a good time, too, it's been. Had a weekend at home with Danny and Sando. Most liberties with Meyers and Lorton. Savings nearly exhausted. Saw quite a bit of the H.J.s. Also, had an evening with Mrs. deMille. More than half the crew's been transferred. All the old hands but me have disappeared. Joe Camera, Nick Maselli, Ray Condon, Archie Archambault, Joe Burke, Herrholz, etc. There are now but 13 of us left in V-3 Division. Lt. Harmen, my officer, was transferred, too, leaving striker Seefried and me alone to run the office. It's all up to me now, no flagship, even, the *Monterey* all alone on the sea, and this is the hurricane season. Chose Seefried to support me, he being the only washed-out cadet who recovered from the shock. So now—all the forecasting's up to me, come hell or high water. For me, the war has just begun. Will be getting up mornings at 0345 for the 8 o'clock forecast. In a terrified way, I kind of like the responsibility. Pulled out of NY this morning, and are now on our way to Naples (not Le Havre) with 450 soldier replacements (not Italian prisoners). We'll return to States with 2,000 U.S. troops. Have six bucks left from the New York blitz. In the safe here, I've 5 pints. On cold nights, what's left of the division can warm up its memories of the Great White Way.

Italian soldiers come aboard in New York.

Returning Italian soldiers to homeland.

MJ, Pompeii.

U.S. troops transfer in Naples for trip home.

2,000 U.S. troops prepare to come aboard in Naples.

Italian soldiers.

Looking off toward Naples *(left)*. Vesuvius *(below)*.

November 27 Yesterday, pulled into Naples, landing liberty from 1 PM to 2300. Naples was once a beautiful city. When one squints, it still is. Sunk my 6 bucks into Italian money. Good exchange. Black Market. What a liberty! The general population seems to have more money than they know what to do with. The trouble is they've nothing to buy. An old man offered me 200 lira for my cigarettes. Gave him 10, for free, and kept 8. Was so grateful, he said, "I take you to daughter. She nice to you." Cigarettes will buy even a child. Those with trinkets to sell were all over us. I got sad. Brought along a dozen handkerchiefs, selling them 2 for a buck. Now I was both sad and ashamed. This morning, turned in my lira, got my 6 bucks back and had nothing but a wad of trinkets and a guilty conscience. With Lorton, Garry, and Mr. Gimble, we took a train to Pompeii. Damned interesting. Back in Naples by 6 PM, we rode around in a horse & buggy for an hour. Dead town, after six, anyway. Our next trip will be to Marseille. At this very moment, there are two hurricanes in the Mediterranean. It's my job to miss 'em, or at least their eyes. Must do some fast research.

Naples, Italy

Bill Grant, driving, who was lost overboard on return cruise from Naples, and Sig Alman, rear left, in New York, November 1945.

[courtesy Sig Alman]

December 6 Pulled into Norfolk today, following a most memorable voyage. Storms all over the place, and seas so high that my friend, Grant, radarman, was swept overboard, and lost. He'd just become engaged. Was able to dodge four hurricanes, their centers, anyway. Terrific seas, though, and high winds, rain, fog, and all the rest of it that can raise hell with a forecaster's life. The Captain and I practically lived on the squarkybox, bridge to aerology, he having complete faith in me (that's how slow he is), and too little in his navigator, a commander. He never questioned a word, however reluctant at times to suggest a certain course and speed. The navigator was sore at *both* of us. It was incredible. For three nights no sleep at all. It was "James, James, James" for five days. One officer remarked, "All that old bastard believes in is James and his Bible." Another one said, "Well, James, it seems you're second in command. What the hell is this navy coming to?" Old salt officers said they'd never seen anything like it, a captain disregarding his navigator's advice for that of an enlisted man's. Once it was, "James, one of the lifeboats is coming loose. What shall I do?" I said, "Slow down, Captain, to 7 knots, and take a SE course." Immediately, he'd order his navigator to follow instructions. I found that very uncomfortable. Got lots of ribbing from

Bob Myers, Orlan Lorton, MJ and Ray Condon, Norfolk, Virginia.

Radar and Air Plot. Well, anyway, we're now safely in port. Last night, he got on the squarkybox, and asked if James was there. "No sir," said Seefried, "I believe he's hit the sack. Shall I get him?" "I'm afraid so, I must speak to him." I came up, squarked a little comfort on the box, and that was that. "Thanks very much, and goodnight, James." Well, that may all sound ordinary enough to civilian ears. Extraordinary is nearer the truth. It's just that that sort of thing never happens. Apparently it did.

December 10 Sandy's birthday. Norfolk's a pretty good liberty town. Richmond's better. Five of us holed up in a dinky hotel. Good bars. Christmas will be at sea, on way to Naples, and New Year's in Norfolk, and that will be that, for that's when the ship is put to rest, retired. Though I'll not miss the life, thank God I went to sea.

December 23 A couple of days ago, pulled into Naples, landing shore patrol duty with Lorton—from noon till 11:30. God, was I tired. Must have walked twelve miles. There was liberty the next day, and sold cigarettes. After making 2500 lira, went to an APO[1] to exchange it for a 25 buck money order. We're now on our way back to Norfolk. May leave the ship the very day we arrive. Goodbye, *Monterey*, and good luck.

1. Army Post Office.

MJ on shore patrol in Naples.

Orlan Lorton and Bob Meyers, Naples.

Lorton and MJ, Naples.

MJ, Naples.

December 28 Have had an amusing time with the Captain. The other day I underestimated the wind. Over the squarkybox, he snapped, "C.I.C. from bridge. Have James report to me." This was the first time he'd ever actually summoned me. "James, you forecasted 13 to 17 knots. They're now 48." "They're 32, Captain." "They're 48," he repeated, "I just worked it up in my head." "Thirty-two, I'm quite sure," I replied. He was now beginning to get sore. "Forty-eight," he said, again. "Well, I guess they're higher than I thought." "You're damned right they are," he snapped. "This forecast is useless," and with that he tore it up into little pieces, dropping them on the deck. "Look at it," he cried, "that's your forecast! It's on the deck! It's worthless!" He's pointing at the deck. "Look, look!" When he was through, I said that forecasting's an inexact science, and left. The next day, he was on the box again. "Good morning, James," he said. "*This* time you've hit it on the head. Over and out." Got quite a ribbing. Yesterday, he and the Executive Officer walked into Aerology. "James, we're going to have a council of war," whereupon he demanded that I tell him precisely how fast he could go for the remainder of the trip—so that he could send in his E.T.A. that afternoon, and with all of *three* days to go! Well, what with possible storms and all, that's *im*possible. Also, it's the navigator's job. After telling him that if we cut down to 14 knots tomorrow, and picked up to 20 in the evening, and to 24 the next day, etc. etc., we settled on an E.T.A. If we miss, it's my ass. We should pull in on the 30th. Passed my physical today. Blood pressure high—otherwise fine.

January 31 On New Year's Day at 9 in the morning, I got into a whaleboat with 40 others, and headed for the shore. A few friends saw me off. Became wistful as the ship got lost in the background. More than I can say went through my mind. Bunked at Norfolk Receiving Station until the 7th. Met some friends first night in town, and had a high time. Following night, returned to the ship for a little visit, but she'd pulled out for Philly. Bussed it

Boarding the whaleboat.

Pulling away from the *Monterey*.

to Boston for a physical exam. High blood pressure, again. To get out, had to sign a paper forgiving the government of all responsibility. My pleasure. Was released at 3 PM of the 10th, precisely 3 years, 3 months, and 19 days after joining. Met Archie, Condon, and Maselli in the Fargo Building, and we fooled around for awhile. Met Danny in Boston, at the Lefferts', and was home before 9. This is the end. Have been out now for nearly three weeks, and I do miss the ship at times. Am restless, and Dad's not well at all. Would like to get into a car and drive around for awhile. Dan's here till March, when he takes off for San Francisco, Sando's to Yale in Feb. Dad's sick with his heart.[1] Mum's the same as ever, though how she can be, I don't know. So that's that. It was quite a war.

1. He was to die a month later.

Off and away.

Looking back.

Appendix

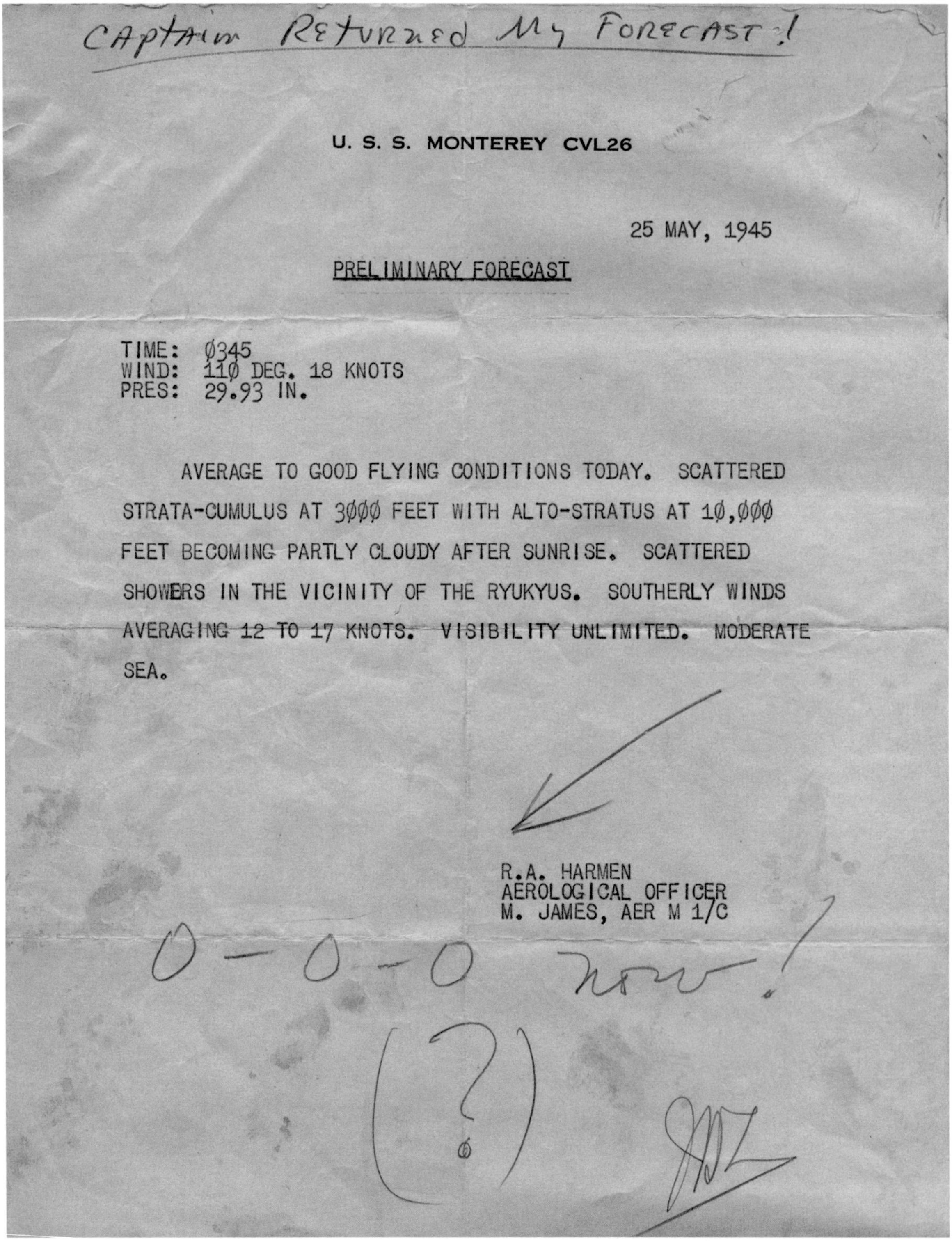

Captain Returned My Forecast !

U. S. S. MONTEREY CVL26

25 MAY, 1945

PRELIMINARY FORECAST

TIME: Ø345
WIND: 11Ø DEG. 18 KNOTS
PRES: 29.93 IN.

AVERAGE TO GOOD FLYING CONDITIONS TODAY. SCATTERED STRATA-CUMULUS AT 3ØØØ FEET WITH ALTO-STRATUS AT 1Ø,ØØØ FEET BECOMING PARTLY CLOUDY AFTER SUNRISE. SCATTERED SHOWERS IN THE VICINITY OF THE RYUKYUS. SOUTHERLY WINDS AVERAGING 12 TO 17 KNOTS. VISIBILITY UNLIMITED. MODERATE SEA.

R.A. HARMEN
AEROLOGICAL OFFICER
M. JAMES, AER M 1/C

0-0-0 now!

(?)

A forecast of mine returned by Capt. Lyon for inaccuracy ('0-0-0' refers to poor visibility).

DEPARTMENT DUTY OFFICERS:

Air	Lt. Cosby	Sunrise 0511
Gunnery	Capt. Price	Sunset 1727
Engineering	Lt. Ranney	VOTING DAY
C & R	Lt. Mallek	
Communications	Lt. Scott	
Medical	Lt. Comdr. Sullivan	
Supply	Lt. Offinger	
Air Group 28	Lt. (jg) Cheney	

PLAN OF THE DAY

2345 Relieve the watch, 2nd section.
0300 Relieve the watch, 3rd section.
0400 Reveille. Stand by for Dawn Alert.
0410 Announce state of weather.
0420 General Quarters. Set Condition Able Modified. Tend openings.
0450 Secure all Mess Cooks and Steward's Mates for breakfast.
0500 Set Condition Baker.
0511 Sunrise. Light ship. Set Condition 23. Mess Gear. Sweep down all compartments and passageways.
0520 Serve breakfast in all messes for two hours.
0700 Relieve the watch, 4th section. Muster Div. P.O's.
0730 Turn to. Muster on stations. 40 hand provision breakout working party report to CCS DUNN in Forward Starboard Messing Compartment.
0800 Launch Aircraft per Air Department Schedule.
0830 Late Hammocks for mid watch. VOTING - Crew's Library.
0945 Sweep down all compartments and passageways.
1045 Mess Gear. 1st section eat early.
1100 Serve dinner for crew. Serve lunch for officers.
1145 Relieve the watch, 1st section.
1200 Turn to.
1230 VOTING - Crew's Library.
1545 Relieve the watch, 2nd section. Sweep down all compartments and passageways.
1655 (Approx) Prepare to darken ship.
1715 Mess Gear, 3rd section eat early.
1727 (Approx) Sunset. Darken ship.
1730 Serve supper for crew. Serve dinner for officers.
1745 Relieve the watch, 3rd section.
1810 (Approx) Gunnery Department Set Condition 22.
1945 Relieve the watch, 4th section.

NOTES:

1. Provision breakout working party.
   Gunnery - 15 hands.
   Air - 15 hands.
   Engineers - 10 hands.

2. Today is Voting Day for those executing Federal Ballots. A special memorandum on the subject has been published by the Commanding Officer.

3. Found - In the vicinity of the Quarter Deck - civilian type raincoat. Owner may contact Lt. West.

4. CONSERVE FRESH WATER!! or as JAMES, AerM2c says, "The showers will be turned off ten minutes ago".

Plan for November 7, 1944.

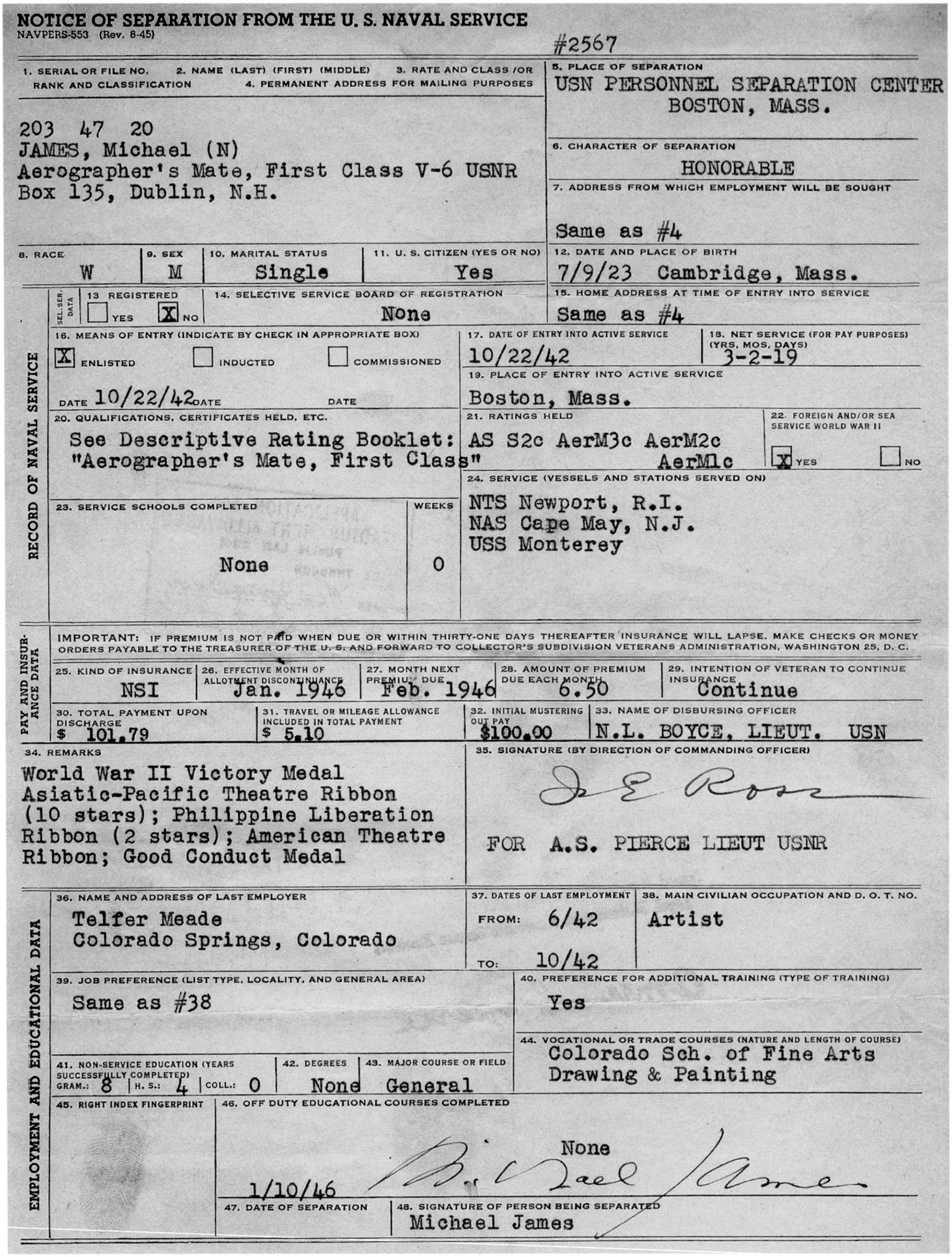

NOTICE OF SEPARATION FROM THE U. S. NAVAL SERVICE
NAVPERS-553 (Rev. 8-45)

#2567

1. SERIAL OR FILE NO. 2. NAME (LAST) (FIRST) (MIDDLE) 3. RATE AND CLASS/OR RANK AND CLASSIFICATION 4. PERMANENT ADDRESS FOR MAILING PURPOSES

203 47 20
JAMES, Michael (N)
Aerographer's Mate, First Class V-6 USNR
Box 135, Dublin, N.H.

5. PLACE OF SEPARATION
USN PERSONNEL SEPARATION CENTER
BOSTON, MASS.

6. CHARACTER OF SEPARATION
HONORABLE

7. ADDRESS FROM WHICH EMPLOYMENT WILL BE SOUGHT
Same as #4

8. RACE: W
9. SEX: M
10. MARITAL STATUS: Single
11. U. S. CITIZEN (YES OR NO): Yes
12. DATE AND PLACE OF BIRTH: 7/9/23 Cambridge, Mass.

RECORD OF NAVAL SERVICE

SEL. SER. DATA
13 REGISTERED: [ ] YES [X] NO
14. SELECTIVE SERVICE BOARD OF REGISTRATION: None
15. HOME ADDRESS AT TIME OF ENTRY INTO SERVICE: Same as #4

16. MEANS OF ENTRY (INDICATE BY CHECK IN APPROPRIATE BOX)
[X] ENLISTED [ ] INDUCTED [ ] COMMISSIONED
DATE 10/22/42 DATE DATE

17. DATE OF ENTRY INTO ACTIVE SERVICE: 10/22/42
18. NET SERVICE (FOR PAY PURPOSES) (YRS, MOS, DAYS): 3-2-19
19. PLACE OF ENTRY INTO ACTIVE SERVICE: Boston, Mass.

20. QUALIFICATIONS, CERTIFICATES HELD, ETC.
See Descriptive Rating Booklet:
"Aerographer's Mate, First Class"

21. RATINGS HELD
AS S2c AerM3c AerM2c
AerM1c

22. FOREIGN AND/OR SEA SERVICE WORLD WAR II: [X] YES [ ] NO

23. SERVICE SCHOOLS COMPLETED: None — WEEKS: 0

24. SERVICE (VESSELS AND STATIONS SERVED ON)
NTS Newport, R.I.
NAS Cape May, N.J.
USS Monterey

PAY AND INSURANCE DATA

IMPORTANT: IF PREMIUM IS NOT PAID WHEN DUE OR WITHIN THIRTY-ONE DAYS THEREAFTER INSURANCE WILL LAPSE. MAKE CHECKS OR MONEY ORDERS PAYABLE TO THE TREASURER OF THE U. S. AND FORWARD TO COLLECTOR'S SUBDIVISION VETERANS ADMINISTRATION, WASHINGTON 25, D. C.

25. KIND OF INSURANCE	26. EFFECTIVE MONTH OF ALLOTMENT DISCONTINUANCE	27. MONTH NEXT PREMIUM DUE	28. AMOUNT OF PREMIUM DUE EACH MONTH	29. INTENTION OF VETERAN TO CONTINUE INSURANCE
NSI	Jan. 1946	Feb. 1946	6.50	Continue

30. TOTAL PAYMENT UPON DISCHARGE	31. TRAVEL OR MILEAGE ALLOWANCE INCLUDED IN TOTAL PAYMENT	32. INITIAL MUSTERING OUT PAY	33. NAME OF DISBURSING OFFICER
$ 101.79	$ 5.10	$100.00	N.L. BOYCE, LIEUT. USN

34. REMARKS
World War II Victory Medal
Asiatic-Pacific Theatre Ribbon
(10 stars); Philippine Liberation
Ribbon (2 stars); American Theatre
Ribbon; Good Conduct Medal

35. SIGNATURE (BY DIRECTION OF COMMANDING OFFICER)
J. E. Ross
FOR A.S. PIERCE LIEUT USNR

EMPLOYMENT AND EDUCATIONAL DATA

36. NAME AND ADDRESS OF LAST EMPLOYER
Telfer Meade
Colorado Springs, Colorado

37. DATES OF LAST EMPLOYMENT: FROM: 6/42 TO: 10/42
38. MAIN CIVILIAN OCCUPATION AND D. O. T. NO.: Artist

39. JOB PREFERENCE (LIST TYPE, LOCALITY, AND GENERAL AREA): Same as #38
40. PREFERENCE FOR ADDITIONAL TRAINING (TYPE OF TRAINING): Yes

41. NON-SERVICE EDUCATION (YEARS SUCCESSFULLY COMPLETED) GRAM.: 8 H. S.: 4 COLL.: 0
42. DEGREES: None
43. MAJOR COURSE OR FIELD: General
44. VOCATIONAL OR TRADE COURSES (NATURE AND LENGTH OF COURSE)
Colorado Sch. of Fine Arts
Drawing & Painting

45. RIGHT INDEX FINGERPRINT
46. OFF DUTY EDUCATIONAL COURSES COMPLETED: None

47. DATE OF SEPARATION: 1/10/46
48. SIGNATURE OF PERSON BEING SEPARATED: Michael James

My notice of separation from the Navy, January 1946.

History of USS *Monterey*:

DAYTON (CL-78) was laid down 29 December 1941 by the New York Shipbuilding Corp., Camden, New Jersey; reclassified CV-26 on 27 March 1942; renamed Monterey 31 March 1942; launched 28 February 1943; sponsored by Mrs. P.N.L. Bellinger; and commissioned 17 June 1943, Capt. Lestor T. Hundt in command.

Monterey was reclassified CVL-26 on 15 July 1943, shortly after commissioning, and, after shakedown, departed Philadelphia for the western Pacific. She reached the Gilberts 19 November 1943, in time to help secure Makin Island. She took part in strikes on Kavieng, New Ireland, 25 December, as part of TG 37.2, and supported the landings at Kwajalein and Eniwetok until 8 February 1944. The light carrier then operated with TF 58 during raids in the Carolines, Marianas, northern New Guinea, and the Bonins from February through July 1944. During this time she was also involved in the Battle of the Philippines Sea on 29 and 30 April.

Monterey then sailed to Pearl Harbor for overhaul, departing once again on 29 August. She launched strikes against Wake Island on 3 September, then joined TF 38 and participated in strikes in the southern Philippines and the Ryukyus. October through December 1944 were spent in the Philippines, supporting first the Leyte, and then the Mindoro landings.

Though enemy planes had been unable to damage Monterey, she did not complete her first full year of service unscathed. In December, she steamed into the path of a howling typhoon, with winds over 100 knots. At the height of the storm, which lasted 2 days, several planes tore loose from their cables, causing several fires on the hangar deck. Monterey arrived Bremerton, Wash., for overhaul, in January 1945. She rejoined TF 58 and supported Okinawa operations by launching strikes against Nansei Shoto and Kyushu from 9 May through 1 June. She rejoined TF 38 for the final strike against Honshu and Hokkaido from 1 July to 15 August.

She departed Japanese waters 7 September, having embarked troops at Tokyo, and steamed home, arriving New York City 17 October. Monterey left behind an impressive and enviable war record. Her planes sank five enemy warships, and damaged others. She was responsible for the destruction of thousands of tons of Japanese shipping, hundreds of planes, and vital industrial complexes. She was assigned "Magic Carpet" duty, and made several voyages between Naples and Norfolk. She decommissioned 11 February 1947, and was assigned to the Atlantic Reserve Fleet, Philadelphia Group.

With the outbreak of hostilities in Korea, Monterey recommissioned 15 September 1950. She departed Norfolk 3 January 1951, and proceeded to Pensacola, Fla., where she operated for the next 4 years under the Naval Training Command, training thousands of naval aviation cadets, student pilots, and helicopter trainees. Between 1 and 11 October 1954, she took part in a flood rescue mission in Honduras. She departed Pensacola 9 June 1955, and steamed to rejoin the Atlantic Reserve Fleet, Philadelphia Group. She decommissioned 16 January 1956. Reclassified AVT-2 on 15 May 1959, she remains berthed at Philadelphia into 1969.

Monterey received 11 battle stars for World War II service.

[*Dictionary of Naval Fighting Ships*, Vol. IV (1969), p. 427]

Letter from my Air Officer, Lt. Robert Olwell

5 November, 1986
87 Sausalito, Calif.

Dear Mike,

Thanks for the lovely evening. It always seems so short. AND for the diary! Are you sure that I can keep it?

I read it in one swoop—with much pleasure. One result that I can see from such a thing, especially when it records, sporadically, events: the great common denominator is missing—the appalling boredom which overlay everything, like a stale sauce. Without it, we seem like bloody heroes, with flaming Bettys out every porthole, punctuated only by worms in the flour. That's another advantage of having been an officer; the worms were there just the same, but no ensign cooks to tell us about them.

Speaking of portholes (here I go), I was in the wardroom having some coffee while standing at an open porthole (we were in Leyte). Framed like a picture out the port was all the fleet, with the Randolph in the middle. As I was vacantly looking out, a P38, flathatting by it at very low altitude...only a few feet above the water, tried a slow roll, and instead, dove right into the Randolph. At first I thought I was seeing things, but finally decided it had to be a kamikaze, called the bridge to call general quarters, and generally made a fool of myself. End of anecdote.

Another thing it really brought back with a rush was our practically paranoid determination to get back to the States for an overhaul. I remember standing near Traua as he was leaning over a table in Air Plot, and a heavy "crrump" sound was heard; he didn't even look up, but muttered, "I hope it's a bomb, I hope it's a bomb!"

I was blissfully unaware of the apparently constant trail of torpedoes passing. I saw only one, the one that zipped past us and hit the Canberra square. The whole Formosa episode was quite depressing, what with the wind, and making smoke, and all the planes coming in at once like they ought to—instead of the old one by one. I really thought we were for it. Especially as we had been assigned to escort the Canberra. I went down to the ward room and played the piano VERY loud when I got word that another CVL had been detailed to it...coward that I am.

I've now read it all again, enjoying it even more. I remember after that first time we shot down a Betty, and every one in the ward room had a completely different story of the event ten minutes after it happened...talk about the Ring and the Book.... Very funny stories about Captain Lyon; he really was an ass.... I remember his ordering flight deck calisthenics when we first left Bremerton, at sea! Suddenly we lost power, and Lyons sagged into his exec's arms...do something! Who can get us started again? When the exec pointed out someone doing pushups, calisthenics were abruptly dropped. Your Atlantic stories were great too. I had no idea that as many people as you describe dropped overboard. I still have nightmares about Danks, the arresting gear man who was swept off by a cable being discarded. I do know that two cans looked for him for an hour.

What I remember most was the strange things that seemed to happen to time; things seemed to last forever, the States were almost in a never never land, probably didn't exist anymore. When we got back at last, it seemed so strange that I was glad to start out again, to crawl back into the sullen cocoon where the horrors were more familiar. When the ship was in New York I was on the Franklin, and was visiting a friend's girl friend's house when the air groups flew up Manhatten, low enough for me to see the air group number of the Monterey as I stood on the roof. For some reason I wept.

And to think that all the time there was this little bomb in your safe? We might just be getting out of Portsmouth[1] about now. Thanks for the kind thoughts anyway. I'm glad I didn't mention to you at the time—that I too was a busted-out cadet, but pre-war, so I was sent home to be recomissioned later, finally getting to sea by way of the arresting gear school; I might have been on your shit list with the other wretches; in fact I know I would have been just as difficult as they were. Oh well, like the Monterey, I was lucky...to have experienced it, and to have had the pleasure of someone to talk to about sensible things in the process.

So much for memory lane. I'm reading a lovely book, the second one of Shaw's letters. What a delight, and such a strange thing that such a crystal mind and such a funny one should (much later than these letters) finally ends up a cantankerous nut. Speaking as one well on his way to that very end, thanks again for your company and for this splendid reminder of that other world.

Best regards from us both
(Signed Bob and Masie)

1. Navy Brig.

Book designed by Henry and Robertson James
Typeset in Adobe Caslon Pro
Printed at The Stinehour Press, Lunenburg, Vermont
Bound at Acme Bookbinding, Charlestown, Massachusetts

L-41027-3 **LOCATION OF STORM'S CENTER WITH RESPECT TO SHIP'**

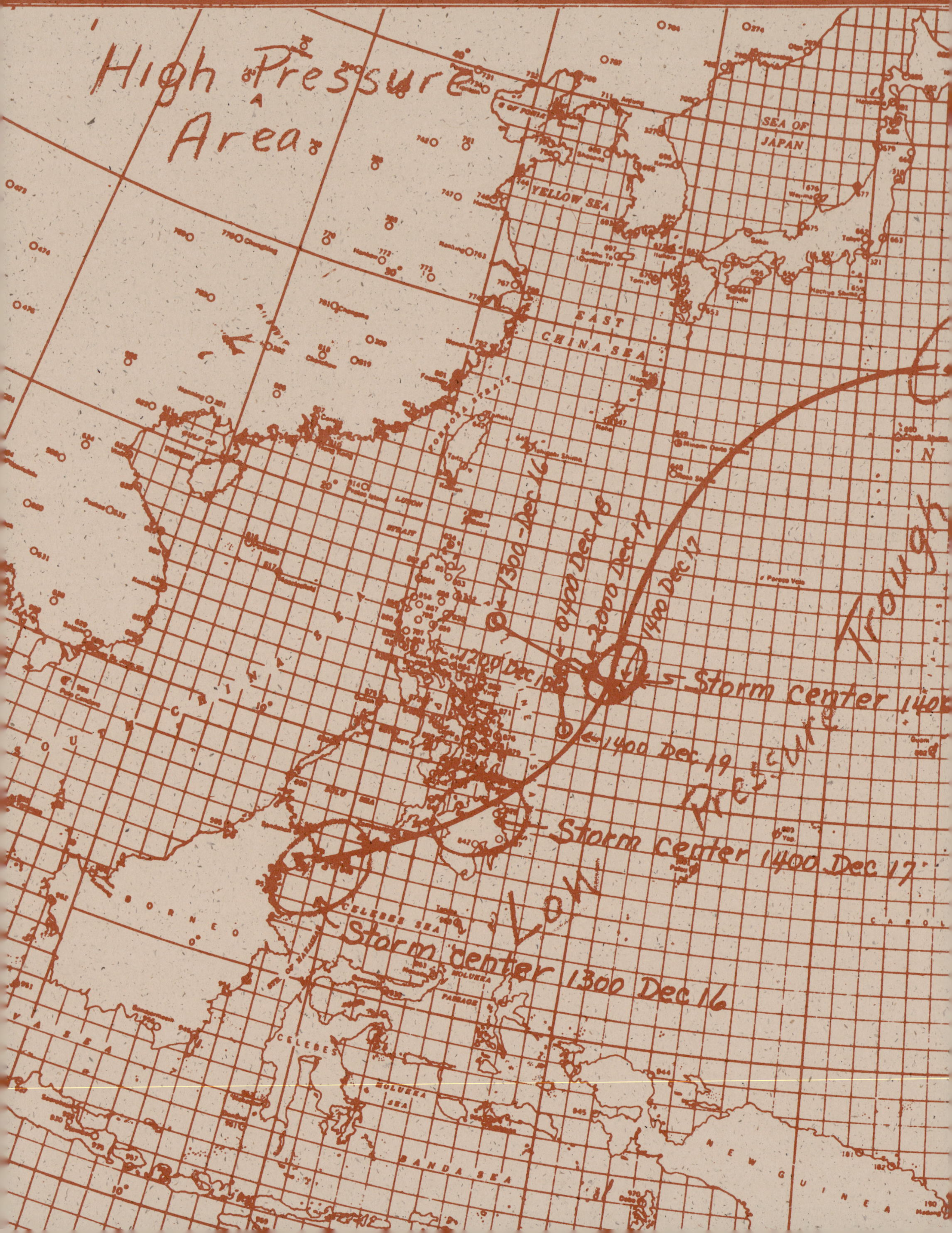